BRATPROOFING
YOUR CHILDREN

BRATPROOFING YOUR CHILDREN

How to Raise Socially and Financially Responsible Kids

Lewis D. Solomon and
Janet Stern Solomon

Skyhorse Publishing

Skyhorse Publishing books may be purchased in bulk at special discounts for sales promotion, corporate gifts, fund-raising, or educational purposes. Special editions can also be created to specifications. For details, contact the Special Sales Department, Skyhorse Publishing, 307 West 36th Street, 11th Floor, New York, NY 10018 or info@skyhorsepublishing.com.

Skyhorse® and Skyhorse Publishing® are registered trademarks of Skyhorse Publishing, Inc.®, a Delaware corporation.

Visit our website at www.skyhorsepublishing.com.

10 9 8 7 6 5 4 3 2 1

Library of Congress Cataloging-in-Publication Data is available on file.

ISBN: 978-1-62087-576-6

Printed in the United States of America

To our son, Michael.

CONTENTS

ACKNOWLEDGMENTS

Our thanks to Lewis J. Saret, who suggested the idea for this book. We also want to posthumously thank Rabbi Morris Lichtenstein, whose focus on character development enlightened our path.

Note: The names used in this book are pseudonyms. We also occasionally changed the genders of named individuals.

INTRODUCTION

This is a book about the human aspects of wealth—
your wealth and its impact on your children. It will
challenge your beliefs about what your money can
and cannot do for your offspring.

As a guide for parents, this book deals with the issues
that you and your "children of affluence" face: the opportunities and the challenges of having and inheriting money.

A brokerage firm recently asked in a large two-page
ad: "Will my kids inherit the work ethic or the wealth ethic?"
Financial privilege can lead to lives of ambition and hard
work for some, while others are strangled by riches, finding only unhappiness, loneliness, a lack of life purpose, or
an attraction to destructive behaviors.

You've probably heard the proverb, "Shirt sleeves to
shirt sleeves in four generations." The first generation
works hard and creates a fortune, often doing it without
significant changes in values or lifestyle. The second generation spends lavishly and joins charitable boards, so the
fortune plateaus and begins to dissipate. The third generation does not work and consumes the family fortune;

the fourth generation returns to hard work and seeking the family fortune.

Perhaps you know a family like the Morgans. Randy, the grandson of the founder of the family business, went to a local banker seeking a loan. The banker exclaimed, "You're a Morgan. Tens of millions of dollars have flowed through your family's hands over the past decades."

"That's correct," Randy replied. "My grandfather built a very successful business. But my father and his siblings sought a new lifestyle, making ever-increasing demands on the family's resources. They sat on the boards of numerous charities and gave generously. What started out as one-time special charitable projects turned into annual commitments. The Morgans became part of high society and developed a pattern of spending on designer clothes, expensive cars, and very lavish parties. Cash flowed out; investments had to be sold. On my father's death, we were left with less than twenty percent of the original family fortune. Now I need a loan. I'll put up Morning Glory, the family estate, which was left to me."

After listening attentively, the banker sadly shook his head. "No. You have mortgaged Morning Glory to the hilt and there is no safety margin. We would be underwater if we needed to foreclose."

A growing number of Americans have accumulated more than enough money to live comfortably. As adults, their children may enjoy the opportunity to pursue their passions as careers and not work merely to pay the monthly bills. One of the advantages of privilege is that it allows for a considerable measure of individual flexibility, and even the freedom from having to work. But privilege has its dark side.

For high-net-worth families, the burden of uncertainty and insecurity that comes from the fear of poverty is lifted. When money is not a concern, you must be more certain about your own beliefs and be willing to act accordingly in raising your children. One of the biggest challenges of wealth is its impact on future generations.

You are probably aware of affluent parents who provided their children with every possible material luxury, only to see them struggle to lead productive lives as adults. They may be unable to retain employment, lack personal passions, and focus only on spending. Some develop serious substance abuse problems. Others continue to live at home, still dependent on their parents.

Parents, especially affluent parents, must be careful not to create "leeches." Leeches come in many forms:

- The **good student leech** excels in studying, often at the best prep schools and most prestigious universities, achieving numerous degrees. The problem is that he continues to acquire one degree after another, living the relaxed student life, while the bank of Mom and Dad pays tuition and living expenses.

- The **crisis leech** seems to find drama at every turn, returning home with an unwanted pregnancy, a wrecked car, an eviction, an unexpected job loss, or some other crisis that requires Mom and Dad to come to the rescue.

- The **addict leech** rotates through a seemingly endless cycle of drug or alcohol binges, rehab, and jail

time. He returns to the family home in between
one stage and the inevitable next.

- The **lazy leech** enjoys sleeping all day and partying all night, seemingly undisturbed by the absence
  of a career or any meaningful occupation.

All these leeches have inherited the "wealth ethic"
instead of the "work ethic."

Every family has its challenges where children are
involved. However, the well-meaning substitution of material goods for responsible child-rearing remains an ill-
fated, familiar pattern in many wealthy families.

Children given too much, too soon, often grow to
become adults who experience difficulty coping with life's
challenges and disappointments. Their distorted sense of
entitlement often gets in the way of success in relationships and in the workplace. Overindulgence often results
in self-centeredness and self-absorption.

Instant material gratification coupled with a focus on
external appearance and emotional deprivation often lead
to low self-worth and self-confidence; an inability to delay
gratification or tolerate frustration; impatience and demands when desires are not immediately fulfilled; an absence of motivation and drive; or an identity crisis marked
by a lack of purpose and difficulty in trusting and forming
lasting relationships, particularly intimate ones.

You want to raise thriving human beings in the next
(and succeeding) generations. You want your children to
grow up to be hardworking, emotionally mature adults,
comfortable in social settings with the nonrich, inclined

to philanthropy, and knowledgeable about investments. You want to raise kids with positive character traits, such as a sense of purpose in life, a sense of direction, and the knowledge that financial privilege is a responsibility. Wealth brings opportunities and corresponding responsibilities on a different scale.

THIS BOOK WILL help you make sure that your kids grow up to be productive, motivated, responsible adults, able to handle life's realities despite having the means to shirk everyday tasks. It will help you to bratproof your kids against becoming self-centered materialists—people who are spoiled, arrogant, and unmotivated, with feelings of entitlement and attitudes of superiority. It will guard against their turning to tragic lives of addiction, drug overdose, or even suicide.

This book will help you to face two challenges: first, protecting your children from the potentially negative influences of your wealth by instilling positive character traits; and second, protecting your wealth from being destroyed by children and grandchildren who are unprepared to handle substantial assets (given that taxes and other external factors may eat away at a family fortune). In addition to preparing wealth for the family, you need to prepare the family for wealth.

PART I

How to Protect Your Children from the
Potentially Negative Influences of Your Wealth

1 Your Responsibilities in Raising Your Children: Five Rules to Remember

Children are one of the greatest delights in life. They are not only dearest to us in the world, but also messengers of joy.

With the first word your child utters and the first step he or she takes, your joy grows ever stronger. However, children are not only given to you to serve as a source of joy and to replenish your hopes. They also impose an enormous responsibility on you as a parent.

The moment a child enters the world, he or she awakens in our hearts a wellspring of love. This "love at first sight" continues throughout the life of each of your offspring, who must experience the feeling of being loved unconditionally—without any performance requirement, whether academic, athletic, musical, or social. Don't substitute material indulgence for nurturing. More "stuff" does not equal more emotional sustenance. Let each child know that you think he or she is special. Children must feel loved and valued.

Ask each, "How do you know I love you?" A child may not see what you consider to be signs of love, so listen to what he or she says and strive to modify your behavior. Small changes may significantly impact a child's view of your love. Try to close the gap between what you intend to express as love and a child's interpretation of your words and deeds.

RULE 1
Always provide your children with your unconditional love and caring.

ONCE CHILDREN COME into this world, parents have a responsibility to love. With love comes duty. Affirm and accept each child for who he or she is. Be accepting and supportive of each one's uniqueness. Accept every aspect of his or her being. Avoid being a "stage mom" or "sports dad," putting the achievement you seek over unconditional love for a child who would prefer to read a book alone or play simple games with a friend.

You may discover that your children may give you unhappiness and trouble. The unpleasantness you get from your children may result, in large part, from the fact that your children received negative influences in their formative years. If this is the case, you as a parent may have much to do to reverse the effects of these negative influences.

The challenge of modern parenthood is especially great for the affluent. You can provide your children with an abundance, if not an overabundance, of material goods. Yet without boundaries from infancy on, children frequently grow up to be spoiled, arrogant brats.

We are from the no-spoiling (or very limited spoiling) school of child-rearing. Affluent parents can bratproof their offspring, although they are wealthy enough to spoil them rotten. Keeping your eye fixed firmly on your children's future means ensuring their long-term happiness, sometimes at the expense of their pleasure in the present.

RULE 2
You are not mean if you discipline your children. Firm, consistent discipline matters.

WHEN OUR SON was two years old and we were traveling across country by car, we stopped for dinner one evening in a nice restaurant. Our usually well-behaved son began acting up even before we had ordered, to the annoyance of other diners. Being a responsive mother, I firmly picked him up, walked with him out to the car and strapped him into his car seat. I leaned over and said quietly but very firmly, "Dad and I want to have dinner and we want you to be with us, but not if you make so much noise. Do you want to stay in the car by yourself or come back inside with me and behave? If you don't behave we will never take you to another restaurant again."

Now, both of these were idle threats; I never would have left him alone in the car, nor would I have refused to take him to another restaurant, but he was two. He understood that I was angry, and he believed me. We returned to the restaurant and had a very peaceful meal, although I got a few curious stares when we quietly returned to our seats.

Provide a predictable, secure home for your children. They need clear, consistently enforced rules, which include a respectful attitude. Select and enforce meaningful consequences, specific and reasonable, whether financial, social or sports activities, or loss of dining out privileges. Ahead of time, inform your children of the consequences of any negative behavior; immediately and calmly impose the penalty, if required. When they ask, your children deserve a reasonable, age-appropriate explanation for your boundaries and sanctions, thereby enabling them to make the choice to behave in an appropriate manner in the future because they understand the rules and the consequences.

Although children need firm discipline, focus on their acts, not on the individual; criticize the behavior, not the child. Focus your discipline on the undesired behavior, and convey your displeasure in neutral terms. A child repeatedly called "stupid" will likely come to believe it. Children are rarely stupid, although their behavior may occasionally cause a parent to wonder. They are just being children.

Children want firm discipline. They need limits on their behavior. They feel better, more secure when they live with a defined structure. Impose a regular bedtime and reasonable curfews. Do not tolerate rude behavior anywhere or bow to every demand. Do not make your home a child-centered place, where everyone automatically caters to a child's wishes. Remember your children need you to be their parent, not their best friend. As a parent, be a cheerleader, but do not cave in.

If your children know there are limits and consequences, they will likely behave; they know that if they don't, they will pay the price. You must, however, set boundaries. Don't tell your teenage daughter what she shouldn't do with respect to drinking or illicit drugs and then leave it up to her. Don't tell her, "I won't be upset if you try pot at parties, but not to touch 'hard drugs.'" And don't regale them with stories of your college drinking or drug experimentation. To a teen, it's like saying, "Do anything you want."

You and your spouse need to develop a unified discipline plan you both can support and administer in a consistent manner.

You don't fulfill your parental duties by merely supplying your children with an endless array of material objects, from toys to computers.

RULE 3
Do not pander to every one of your child's material desires.

WE WERE RECENTLY invited to the home of friends to admire their new living room furniture, but when we arrived the sofa, chairs, and floor were covered by a sea of puppets, toys, dress-up costumes, and other children's belongings. Our friends typified many affluent parents who often give their children every advantage. Despite the best of intentions, they raise "wanting machines," who only want more and more material goods. These parents confuse permissiveness with love. Don't give *things* rather than giving yourself.

All the kids in your child's class get extravagant birthday parties—at least, that's what you're told. Your son wants one. Just say, "I do not believe in spending large sums of money on parties. We can afford it, but that isn't how we choose to spend our money." It isn't necessary to hire an elephant for kiddy rides, as one father did, for your son or daughter to celebrate a birthday.

You must learn to deal with a child's craving for some new, costly material object and her insistence that "Everyone has one." It is harder to say "No" when you can afford to say "Yes." But don't breed in your children an enormous sense of entitlement by over-providing material goods. Once you turn the faucet on by giving children their wants rather than their needs, it is hard to turn it off.

Learn to say "No" to the call of expensive toys, clothes, and electronics. When your daughter says, "I want a $300 sweater like Susie's," be prepared to respond, "In this family, we don't wear $300 sweaters." By minimizing the importance of the high-priced, brand-name clothes your children wear, you indicate that your belief system reflects more than material goods do.

On our son's eleventh birthday, he came downstairs crowing, "Only five more years until I get a car!" Our response was that he could have any car he could afford to buy. We promised to pay for car insurance, but told him to start saving birthday checks and other money because he would be paying for the car on his own. He took us seriously, saved his money, and bought his first car at nineteen. Despite being very financially successful after college, he kept that first car he bought with his own money for more than ten years. It had almost 200,000 miles and a lot of dents and dings, but he loved that car as he would never have cared about something we bought for him.

Don't provide more material goods than your children need. We realize that this is difficult in modern-day America, because you don't want to appear miserly. Listen to your children's wishes and their desires to fit in, but stand on your principles. Never lie to your children (Virtue 7, page 71) and tell them you can't afford something when obviously you can.

Remember: Overindulging often leads to an inability to tolerate the discomfort of thwarted instant gratification. Often, these children will not stick to and master tasks, and thereby forgo experiencing the pleasure of achievement. Because life has its ups and downs, it is vitally important for your children to experience delayed gratification and overcome frustration. Children need to experience the inner satisfaction of turning adversity into challenge and then achievement. It contributes to their developing emotional resilience.

RULE 4
"No" belongs in every parent's vocabulary, to be used responsibly.

CHILDREN NEED TO hear the word "No" in order to grow. Say "No" and mean it. Don't worry that your children will dislike you, will throw a tantrum, or will be permanently damaged. Again, both parents must create a united front.

Sometimes a "No," on reasoned reflection bends to a "Yes." Your eight-year-old daughter, wanting to feel grown up, asks for her own cell phone. Realizing that cell phones have emerged as the latest must-have electronic status symbol among elementary schoolers, you say "No." She persists, pointing out a bright red one that features five keys, including keys with icons for speed-dialing parents.

Rational arguments for saying no continue to reverberate in your head: eight-year-olds are rarely ever without adult supervision, cell phones are often lost, batteries quickly run out of power, and so on. However, you're part of a two-career household and cell phones provide an electronic security blanket, an emergency backup system in a post–9/11 world of color-coded threat levels and possible terrorist attacks. You can easily afford to purchase a nice youth-oriented phone plus the prepaid airtime. Ultimately, persuaded by the global-positioning satellite feature that allows you to locate the phone (and presumably your daughter) from another phone, you give in, rationalizing, "It will give me peace of mind, for instance, when she's riding in the school bus. What if the bus driver has a medical emergency or the bus is stranded in the snow?"

However, once you were called a dozen times in four days, the novelty wore off and you weren't called again. "She doesn't use it, but I like knowing it is there." When other children at school saw that your daughter had a cell phone, several, including her best friend, went home and begged for one. You realize that you should have admonished her: "It's a privilege to have a cell phone. Don't advertise it to the other children, especially kids from families who cannot afford one and may be made to feel worse and worse."

RULE 5
Spend time with your children; get to know each of them.

BEYOND THE USUAL obligations such as attending a child's soccer game or a cultural performance, make sure to spend time with each of your children. Play a game together, read to or with them, build something together, go for a walk with them. Often, what children value most about each week is time spent with parents. Lavish each child with the gift of your time. One of the authors vividly recalls the lazy summer weekends he spent fishing with his father and their annual father-son visit to the circus.

To raise children who can and want to successfully take charge of their lives as adults, be present for your children. Give them your scarcest resources—your time and your emotional energy—to provide the full range of unconditional parental love, from affection to setting clear boundaries. Remember Rules 1 and 2, pages 20 and 21. Developing a close, honest relationship with each of your children probably represents the most powerful protection against risky behavior, such as substance abuse or eating disorders.

Dinnertime provides the most convenient, comfortable way to build these connections, especially over the foods your children like. It enables parents to monitor their children's behavior and provides an opportunity to create a sense of belonging to a family unit.

Try to have dinner together with your children as many evenings as possible each week. Obstacles exist, of course, including late working hours of one (or both) parents and activities that overlap with dinnertime. Don't schedule another meeting for yourself or another activity for your children at the family dinner hour.

Family dinnertime provides structure, a predictable routine, and a sense of community. It builds family bonds; it should be a relaxing time during which family members can enjoy each other's company. It provides an opportunity for conversation, perhaps about current events, in our noisy, frenzied world. Curb your tendency to preach to your children. Ask questions to draw them out and listen to their answers; try to listen, without criticism, or interruption, even if the thoughts and feelings they express seem trivial. Strive to be knowledgeable about each child's heroes, friends, likes, and dislikes.

The family dinner hour also provides a good opportunity for children to learn table manners, but try not to put a damper on the atmosphere. Avoid unnecessary reprimanding. We realize that it's difficult, but try to share at least some part of the food together so that the gathering retains its power to connect. Not everyone likes to eat the same foods, but the act of sharing food together increases the bonds between family members and the acceptance of each other's different tastes.

Always remember that the best things you give your children is your love and nurturing, not expensive toys, vacations, or automobiles.

No matter how busy you are, try to spend 10 to 15 minutes a day with each of your children, one-on-one and uninterrupted, in person or on the telephone. One child may require more of this private time than another. It may be at bedtime with younger children; for older ones, perhaps walking the dog or in the car on the way to school in the morning. Give each child your undivided attention and let him or her discuss anything he or she wants to, express any opinion, without any negative reaction on your part. Let each know you will listen, thereby creating an environment conducive to ongoing, honest, parent-child communication.

2 The Key to Child Rearing: Impart Seven Positive Character Traits

I nstead of nonjudgmentalism or letting children "do their own thing," which we believe often leads to hedonism and narcissism, we recommend providing strong guidance and standards for your children. Let them learn to differentiate between right and wrong, good and evil. Improving one's character is, in our opinion, the goal of life. Perfection cannot, however, be the expectation.

In thinking about character formation, remember that children evolve through three distinct stages of growth and development: infancy, youth, and adolescence. Although they are always your children, their relationships to you as a parent change as they grow older. In infancy, they belong totally to you. In youth, they belong partly to you and partly to the world; in adolescence they belong mostly to the world and only a small part to you.

In each stage of development, they are, of course, your children. However, they are different beings in each of these periods. Although your children are tied to you in all these stages, with each succeeding stage, their relationship to the world outside the home changes. Through their growth and development, their independence becomes stronger and more assertive.

For purposes of this chapter, as well as Chapters 3 and 4, let's focus on the dependent stage, which comprises the early years of a child's existence, when a child is malleable, ready to be fashioned. It is the most important period in the formation of one's character. Each child is equipped with abilities and potentialities that will bring out the best in him or her if properly cultivated. Through proper training, guidance, and encouragement you can help cultivate those qualities that make for greatness; conversely, erroneous emphasis or negligent care may lead to a life of smallness, if not failure.

The first ten years or so are the most important ones in your children's lives. During these years, the foundation is put in place for all their subsequent years. Because a child is malleable, during the first decade of his or her life, a considerable amount of molding is possible. Thereafter, although a child continues to acquire more knowledge and skills, as discussed in Chapter 11 change in one's habits, although not impossible, becomes more difficult; new things do not take root as quickly; new character traits are often only imparted after a struggle.

Thus, the formative years are the time to implant virtuous qualities, the seeds of good character traits, in your children. We easily recognize from an adult's conduct the quality of nurturing they received during their childhood years. Character, whether positive or negative, results from years of good or bad nurturing. As a parent, strive to implant positive virtues and good qualities in your children. Do not comfort yourself by thinking that they will just grow up to be "decent" people. Do not take for granted that they will learn these beneficial traits without any special parental attention.

Chapters 3 and 4 offer seven key character traits: four personal ones, namely, high self-esteem, joyfulness and optimism, serenity, hard work and thrift; and three interpersonal ones, lovingkindness, forgiveness, and integrity.

Instilling positive character traits in children is tricky. Let us offer several suggestions. The practice of these virtues begins at home. If each is not applied first within your home, then its application elsewhere will not only be more difficult but also of little significance. A virtue practiced at home, for its own sake, not for any ulterior gain, best promotes one's character. Conversely, a virtue practiced as an expedient, in order to gain some desired end, does not enhance one's character or enrich human relationships. For example, have you ever been in a restaurant with a disruptive child? Did that enhance your dining experience? It is easier to require children to be quiet and respectful in a restaurant or someone else's home if the same behavior is required in your own home.

As noted in Chapter 1, begin by demonstrating, through your deeds and words, unconditional love for each of your children. As Shakespeare said, "They do not love who do not show their love." It's not hard to say the words, but words are not enough. Love is shown by caring, doing, remembering, and listening. Remember Rule 1 (page 20). Base your relationship to your children on unconditional love. You raise them and you suffer with them because you love them. Your hearts are tied to theirs. Do not, however, succumb, because of your desire for their immediate pleasure, to encourage the development of tendencies that may prove injurious to them in the long run. Remember Rules 2, 3, and 4 (pages 21, 23, 25).

As a parent, you have a responsibility to furnish each of your children with a proper pattern, with a sound model for each to imitate and follow. Whatever path you wish your child to tread, first walk in the path you wish him or her to go.

Children learn virtues from your behavior. What you do must be consistent with what you tell your children. Teach these seven virtues by example, thereby creating a sound foundation for living. Demonstrate to your children that you take each of these virtues seriously. Remember, you are a role model and if you want them to value money and spend wisely, avoid your own "shopping therapy." Let them see that you do not shop for entertainment, to alleviate loneliness, to dispel boredom, or to relieve depression. Instead, teach them to be knowledgeable and informed consumers when they do need to make a purchase, rather than responding to advertising.

Don't preach one set of character traits, then model another for your children. It's not effective to lecture your kids about not using drugs while you are downing your third or fourth martini. The messages your deeds send to your children may come through even more clearly than the messages you deliver with words.

To impart sound character traits to your children, take a long, hard look at your own life, your own attitudes, behaviors, and priorities. By leading a virtuous life, you have the credibility to train your children to reach that standard. As developed in Chapter 11, you may want to write a family mission statement, a compass designed to help you shape how you lead your life and make your everyday decisions.

Children absorb and observe virtues on a day-to-day basis. Plant character traits at a child's impressionable age, through your own deeds. He or she will never forget what you do in their presence. These acts enter their consciousness and mold their personality and character. Encouraging sound habits at an early age makes a big difference. Don't just talk a good game—play like you mean it.

Children also follow and learn from your mental state, your demeanor, and your expressions. The Kennedy family presents a great commitment to public service without the goal of financial gain, as witnessed by the large number of offspring who have held public office. Likewise, military service, social service, law enforcement and other careers often attract many generations from the same family.

The tongue is a powerful, all-too-often negative, tool. Words you say as a parent are often never forgotten. One of the authors grew up in a family where she was frequently referred to as stupid, dumb, or silly. It took decades before she overcame this stigma and achieved a Ph.D. Following her doctoral graduation, a close friend remarked: "Did you get the doctorate to prove to your mother that you aren't stupid?"

A child learns by imitation. You provide the patterns that a child copies. There is no need to lecture. Generally, you need only give a proper pattern and it will be followed. What you wish a child to remember for life must be given by example.

Guide your children closely, but not oppressively; influence their lives, but do not overpower their will. Lead them onto the right path, but do not force them.

Children learn much more from you than what you intend to teach. In raising children, it is not only what you do for them, but much more importantly what you do in front of them that counts in building their character. In this era of divorce and blended families, there is also an increasing importance of grandparents and step-siblings as role models of behavior and attitude.

As your children mature, so should your expectations for their behavior. As each stage of development unfolds, you can increase each child's level of responsibility. Also, do not shield your children from your mistakes; discuss them openly and constructively so that they learn from your own challenges and disappointments. You not only become more human, but you also present a role model for them.

UNTRAINED AND INEXPERIENCED children look to parental leadership. Chapters 3 and 4 discuss these seven specific virtues—character traits.

Remember: Giving lip service to a character trait is not sufficient. You must care emotionally about each virtue and then act in accordance with it.

3 Four Personal Character Traits: High Self-Esteem, Joyfulness and Optimism, Serenity, Hard Work and Thrift

This chapter presents four personal character traits: high self-esteem, joyfulness and optimism, serenity, and hard work and thrift. After briefly considering the characteristics of each trait, practical techniques to build these traits are presented.

VIRTUE 1
Self-Esteem

CHARACTERISTICS OF THIS TRAIT. Self-esteem rests on self-reliance, self-confidence, and courage. In short, it relies on feeling good about oneself and a belief in one's own potential.

Self-reliance connotes self-trust and self-respect, faith in oneself, in one's thoughts, feelings, and opinions. Self-reliant individuals express their needs, wants, feelings, stand their ground, and trust their own judgment. Self-reliance implies a love of responsibilities and the cultivation of ever greater degrees of responsibility.

Those with high self-esteem approach each task, no matter how small, with self-confidence. They attack a task with trust in their powers and confidence in themselves, bent on achievement.

While envy constantly tempts us to judge our worth in comparison to others, self-confidence invites one to treasure and develop one's own unique gifts and attributes. It's a belief in one's own competence. Having self-confidence means believing that: difficulties cannot stop us; nothing stands between us and our goals; we can cope with life's challenges and make a difference in the world.

Courage represents another aspect of a positive self-image. The courage to be oneself, to create and achieve, to actualize one's ideals by expressing lovingkindness (Virtue 5) to others, by being forgiving (Virtue 6) of others, and being truthful and honest (Virtue 7) with others.

With self-reliance and self-confidence comes courage, the willingness to affirm one's personal integrity in the midst of life's challenges. Courage enables one to overcome life's dangers and hardships. It lets one deal constructively with life's complexities and ambiguities. It enables one to surmount one's fears and worries and defy obstacles.

Children of privilege need to experience life's disappointments and frustrations as well as its joys and successes. They must learn to cope with life's obstacles. A child with self-esteem can face life's challenges with confidence in his or her ability to remain centered and strong. It is one of the best gifts any parent can give a child.

TECHNIQUES TO BUILD SELF-ESTEEM. You can help your children acquire self-esteem; it is not innate. Imparting high self-esteem to your children begins with your possessing a positive self-image and demonstrating it daily. Also, you need to deal with any problems between you and your spouse that create an unstable, dysfunctional family.

Give your children your unconditional love and encouragement (Rule 1, page 20), coupled with boundaries and when needed, firm discipline (Rule 2, page 21), to help them build their self-esteem. Hold, cuddle, and kiss your children, starting at birth, and tell them they're loved and valued. This can continue despite your teenage son moaning "Oh, Mom!" and rolling his eyes. He cannot consciously express it, but at a deeper level he does still want hugs. Self-esteem grows out of this love early in life.

Children must also feel competent in their own abilities. Communicate to your children their worth, competence, desirability, and goodness. Continue to express your unconditional love, whether your children win or lose, succeed or fail. Children fall down, but they learn to walk by getting up again and continuing to try. Celebrate improvements and small successes. Praise each for making an effort; be specific in your praise. Acknowledge and support their attempts; remind them that failure happens to everyone. Reward them verbally for their efforts and they will be less fearful of failure and more willing to try again in the future.

Conversely, do not scold a child for failing, otherwise he or she will more likely view a specific failure as a sign of overall failure. By encouraging a child and praising him or her for trying—for effort, attitude, perseverance—he or she is more likely to see failure as an isolated event and more likely to take sound risks.

It may not be easy to detach yourself and let your children succeed or fail, especially as they try new challenges, whether meeting new people or learning new lessons at school. *Remember*: Detaching fosters self-reliance and self-confidence.

Strive to empower your children. Even a toddler can make decisions and begin to take responsibility for them. Ask: "Do you want to wear a red or a blue shirt?" By empowering him or her, you send a message that he or she is sufficiently important that you value his or her opinions. Move quickly from two choices onto three, then four alternatives. When children are four years old, they generally can handle five or six choices.

Teach your children to gradually embrace decisions and responsibility, particularly, the responsibility to make decisions. Let your children make age-appropriate decisions and learn the consequences of poor choices. By making decisions, especially important ones, for your children you breed passive, dependent adults who are unable to function independently. Children need to make decisions for themselves and learn from their mistakes. If they choose the wrong book or game to take on a long car trip, they will need to learn to be creative in entertaining themselves. They also need to be able to handle and solve their own problems whenever possible.

Self-worth builds on the acceptance of one's perfections and imperfections. Children ought to learn who they are, but do not foster within them a sense of inferiority, which will limit their potential for achievement and success.

A former colleague of ours was born without arms. Her mother had been prescribed thalidomide during her pregnancy before the disastrous side effects of the drug were known. However, her mother raised her daughter to appreciate her intelligence, creativity and other assets. The result was that the daughter became a well-respected expert in her field who could joke about saving money on underarm deodorant since she had no arms.

Do not let any child brood over his or her physical defects. Do not let your children see themselves as inferior to or envious of others because of their weight, height, body image, or physical appearance. Focus on one's bodily competence, not appearance. We realize this is difficult, but as long as the essence of one's mind—one's intellect, one's will, one's spirit—is not impaired, bodily blemishes or defects cannot prevent achievements. Emphasize the importance of the person inside.

Encourage your children to see their positive attributes. Help them search for their positive qualities, their natural gifts and strengths. Assist them in finding good points so that they can draw support from internal sources. Each of us has vast, untapped treasures, physical, mental, emotional, and spiritual.

Discover and bring out each child's unique talents, but do not demand the impossible. Notwithstanding Tiger Woods' father, "sports dads" and "stage moms" have acquired a lot of negative press, with some justification. Do not try to live vicariously through a child; don't push your child to accomplish what you could not achieve. Don't measure your own self-worth by your child's grades, performance in sports or cultural activities, or admission to a prestigious college. Not all children belong in the Ivy League.

While encouraging them to do their best, indicate that it is not necessary to achieve perfection. Do not force them to do too much. Help each focus on one or two things he or she does well and encourage him or her to get involved with that activity. Let each feel successful at an enjoyable activity. *Remember*: All of us generally succeed in activities in which we choose to be involved and enjoy for their own sake—motivation that comes from within.

Celebrate each child's differences. The Jackson family clearly has musical talent, but not all the Jackson children could be stars at the level of Michael or Janet. Recognize that children have various types of intelligence, analytical, creative, emotional, and social, and thus, different learning styles; they also have diverse temperaments and mature differently. Within each, encourage curiosity, creativity, drive, and organization so he or she will strive to reach his or her potential.

Help each set realistic, achievable goals and gradually raise the bar. Strive to see each objectively and encourage each to build his or her competence and try new things, take on greater challenges, and embrace new opportunities. Measure success by how hard a child tries—by one's effort, not one's achievement.

Help each, even younger ones, sort out their unique strengths and weaknesses. Assist your children in understanding and using their unique talents and strengths, and working through or around any weaknesses, bypassing obstacles blocking one's way to success. Children simply cannot be good at everything throughout their K–12 school years. Sooner or later nearly all children will face a situation for which they are not wired.

The young son of an important chemist showed no aptitude at all for any of the sciences. Instead, he was constantly drawing; at a very early age, he loved to go to museums and could quietly admire paintings long before his classmates were mature enough for such an activity. His father disdained this as a waste of time, but his mother encouraged him as much as possible and he eventually became a well-respected art historian.

Draw out each child. Find out each one's interests and dreams. Use that knowledge to stimulate and motivate. Help each find a path for which he or she has a natural affinity and cultivate it. Bring out the best in each child. Encourage the expression of the qualities and abilities that are inherent in him or her.

Be a cheerleader, a motivator, support and encourage each child's natural abilities and interests, but don't push. Avoid unrealistic expectations that fail to consider a child's unique abilities and interests. Let your child know what you admire in him or her. Accept each for who he or she is.

Do not let them give up on their passions, the things that naturally energize and excite them early in life. As they move to adolescence, helping your children find not only their passions but also their purpose in life will enable them to achieve a more meaningful existence. Finding one's purpose in life turns on discovering what makes one feel fulfilled, doing something that is both satisfying and important. Each of us has a unique place in creation; a place that only we can fill. Help each of your children discover what his or her soul yearns for, what his or her heart really wants.

Let your ten- or twelve-year-old begin to dream big. Don't narrow your children's dream by treating them condescendingly. Guide your child with useful information about his or her passions. You likely have the financial ability to fund his or her heart's desires. With loving parents, a supportive environment, and your financial resources, each of your children can take steps toward (and may attain) his or her goals. Teach your children to aim as high as their abilities and potential will carry them.

While encouraging each child's unique talents and abilities, however, let each know that it is important to keep their options open. The budding rock musician in high school may in college want to become a physician.

A lot of harm has been done by the words "Why can't you be more like [*fill in a sibling or other name*]?" Know each child's talents, interests, and passions, so you can nurture them appropriately. Help each find his or her own potential, rather than having him or her struggle to meet your expectations or match a sibling's achievements. Lead each child down a separate road so that he or she does not feel he or she is competing with his or her siblings or children of friends or relatives. Don't create expectations based on comparisons.

Encourage self-esteem at each stage of development as follows:

- During the first year, children form their basic sense of trust from parents' consistent, unconditional love (Rule 1, page 20). Hold your newborns and toddlers often.

- During the second year, children begin to develop a sense of autonomy and independence. Within certain parameters, let a child explore his or her environment in an unstructured way and derive joy from his or her discoveries. Don't be overprotective; this will make your child feel apprehensive, incompetent, or unable to accomplish basic tasks. Also, include children in simple decision making.

- From ages three to five, encourage children, who are becoming persons in their own right, to develop a greater sense of initiative. Also, try to keep punishment to a minimum, but apply loving, firm, consistent discipline when needed (Rule 2, page 21).

- For school-age children, once the child is well settled at school, try to make sure he or she is having enough fun and making contact with children of his or her own age. Do not overload youngsters with too many activities. Do not lock your children into a series of activities you dictate. Focus on what each child does well and have him or her get involved with that. If a child has different talents and interests than you do, encourage him or her. Respect his or her talents and interests. Let him or her feel successful in an endeavor he or she enjoys.

Always compliment your children on their positive behavior and attitude. Tell your children they are terrific just for trying. Give them the confidence to face life's challenges. Children with an "I can do it" attitude will likely have high self-esteem, feel inherently worthwhile, and are more likely to be joyful and optimistic.

VIRTUE 2
Joyfulness and Optimism

AT A BRIDAL shower, the differences between the groom's mother and the bride's mother were starkly evident to all but the bride. As the bride opened each gift, the groom's mother exclaimed: "How beautiful!" or "I love that." At nearly the same time the bride's mother declared, "How ugly," "That is too fragile and will break," or "You will never use that; it's too impractical." Oddly, until the groom's sister mentioned her observations to the bride the next day, the bride had never thought of her mother as a pessimist. She had heard the litany all her life and accepted it as truth.

CHARACTERISTICS OF THESE TRAITS. The greater one's sense of joy and optimism, the greater one's enjoyment of and potential in life and ability to cope with hardships and tragedies, the unexpected setbacks and unforeseen hurdles we all face in life.

Conversely, a pessimistic viewpoint often precludes joyfulness and happiness. It deteriorates one's mind, destroying its fine edge. It limits one's ambition, causing one to lose interest in the vital aspects of life. It often predisposes one to failure.

Pessimism often manifests itself in fear and worry. Fear about the here and now, about how our words or deeds (or others' speech or conduct) will result in sad or painful consequences for us, keeps us down. Worry fills us with many fears about the future, robbing us of our present pleasure.

Laura, now an elderly woman, had some tragedies in her early life, but for the past fifty years she has lived a relatively affluent, healthy, and comfortable life. However, her persistent pessimism keeps her in a near constant state of sadness and a paralysis of negativity, marked by irrational fears. When her out-of-town family announces they are coming to visit, she welcomes the news but imagines car or plane crashes, convinced that there will be a disaster during their travel. By the time the relatives arrive, she has put everyone on edge and will repeat the pattern when they leave, spoiling the visit for everyone. Her relatives' visits become fewer and further apart.

Joy is a weapon against the fear, worry, and pessimism that pervade modern society, unhappily crowding one's life. By carrying joy into maturity, we are able to face life with more courage and less fear, and shut the doors of our hearts and minds on worry and despair.

TECHNIQUES TO BUILD JOYFULNESS AND OPTIMISM. When life gives you lemons, make lemonade. Begin by striving to banish gloom from yourself, particularly at home. Leave your fears and worries behind, never taking them over the threshold of your home. In your home, express cheerful, happy words and feelings. By carrying out this spirit at home, your children will manifest it throughout the day, wherever they are.

Although the pessimism and the emotional depression we see all too often may result from disease, biological factors, such as inherited disturbances in brain chemistry, or psychological factors, help your children learn to cultivate joyfulness and optimism. Teach them to substitute positive life forces for the negative ones. For most of us, we are what we think. Your way of thinking—whether positive or negative—creates the world you see.

Encourage your children to develop optimistic attitudes. Cultivate habits that make for joy. As a parent, think, speak, and act cheerfully. Select an optimistic outlook on life and impart it to your children. Despite adverse circumstances, do not let your spirit droop.

By making joy and optimism your habit, your children will learn from you. Begin each day anew—start fresh. Tell yourself positive things. Smile in the face of seeming calamity. Refill your mind with cheerful thoughts. Do not listen to pessimistic thoughts. Read upbeat books and magazines; watch hopeful TV shows and movies; be in the company of optimistic people. Let your children see how you retain your joyfulness and optimism in the face of disappointment and adverse circumstances.

Teach a child to bring joyfulness and optimism into play whenever a difficult situation arises. You prepare a child to meet life's difficulties in an impenetrable armor. By filling one's mind with optimism, one will not become prey to discouraging influences. Rather, he or she will think in terms of success, of achieving positive goals, in school, in college, and in their careers.

If your children suffer setbacks, whether at school or in relationships with others, let them learn from you.

Let them see how new dreams bloom, bringing forth the fruits of future successes. Let them see that you do not let temporary setbacks slow your momentum or disrupt the pursuit of your goals. Show them that you regroup quickly and find new ways to move forward. Demonstrate that you do not despair, but rather persevere, finding alternative paths to reach your goals. Always remind yourself and your children of one's unique, inner strengths and good qualities, and put them to work.

Parents should watch out for dangerous friends who may be into drugs or other activities from which they want to protect their children. You need to teach your children to be selective in their friends (see Chapter 5). Instruct them to avoid, if possible, anyone who interferes with their joyful, optimistic outlook on life and to seek out the company of cheerful individuals.

For most of us, the power of positive thinking is sufficient, enabling us to overcome hardships or disappointments. Others need to learn the skills of optimism, specifically, the technique of reframing a situation, which involves changing thought patterns and mental habits, not overreacting to situations, in a more structured manner. You may want to read something by Professor Martin E. P. Seligman, a University of Pennsylvania psychologist. Or, you may need to seek out a therapist to help in learning the coping skills of optimism, which focuses on the power of nonnegative thinking—controlling one's attitude toward people or events, unlearning a pessimistic outlook on life, and rewriting one's negative scripts. By altering how one interprets a situation, one learns to turn a seemingly negative event into something positive.

Most of us can teach our children to reframe nearly every situation in order to find the good, not the negative. We can encourage them to have positive expectations and avoid destructive beliefs.

VIRTUE 3
Serenity

WE LIVE IN a fast-paced, electronic, multi-tasking society, where serenity is always available, but often needs to be sought out. As one mother often reminded her son, "When you have tranquility, you have everything; when you lack tranquility, you have nothing."

CHARACTERISTICS OF THIS TRAIT. Peace of mind is requisite to personal happiness and fulfillment. Your self-esteem, your joyfulness and optimism, your efforts at work, flourish on a serene background, a mentally peaceful atmosphere. The importance of inner peace of mind cannot be overestimated.

When we are serene, we express the best of ourselves. Our best qualities, our best virtues assert themselves when we are calm. The wellsprings of lovingkindness and forgiveness open to others.

By living a serene life, our powers function at their best. When we are tranquil, we best express our mental powers. Thoughts come more readily; concentration and powers of memory are at their best.

Peace of mind is essential to accomplishment in life. Lasting achievements are produced when one's inner life is peaceful. Accomplishment bursts forth from a calm mind. We do our best work when our inner life is peaceful.

When we are serene, we better face and solve the challenges life holds for us. A tranquil nature better preserves our physical and emotional well-being.

Strive for tranquility, not anger or envy. Rather, aim for contentment, which keeps one serene; calm mind, warm heart, and compassionate spirit.

Contentment does not connote the passive acceptance of one's situation or attainments. Reach out to achieve your ideals; expand the depths of your mind. Strive to be more loving, forgiving, truthful, and honest in your interactions with others.

TECHNIQUES TO BUILD SERENITY. Serenity must be practiced first in your home; then it will more readily manifest itself elsewhere. Before you return home, allow yourself a period of time to transition from the world of work to the world of your family. Perhaps walk around the block once or twice. Let your children see that you are tranquil, both externally and internally. Avoid a double nature, a calm appearance you show to the world and another nature by which you live your private life.

Train your children to strive for equanimity in the midst of life's storms. Let them see that when you encounter people or events that could justifiably provoke anger or impatience, you remain calm. Show them that you take a breather and wait out the commotion. Let them see that you are not envious of other's wealth or happiness.

Train them in patience—not resignation, but in having hope in the future, despite setbacks, even hardships and calamity. Patience teaches us to wait for a better future, remembering the best will often come even if it is delayed a bit.

In particular, teach your children to be patient with others as long as they are not doing anything illegal, unloving, untruthful, or dishonest. Demonstrate that when you feel agitated you do not unleash your fury on others; rather, you slow down and listen, striving to put yourself in the other person's shoes.

Increasingly, people find it helpful to meditate to restore and maintain tranquility by inducing a relaxed state of being. There are numerous styles of mediation, with various goals in mind. There's no one right way. Let us point out one, the Relaxation Response, a demystified form of meditation, popularized by Herbert Benson, M.D., of the Harvard Medical School in his many books.

Once or twice daily, sit comfortably with your eyes closed. Then, let your muscles relax, starting with your face and working to your feet. Become aware of your breath as you breathe in and out. Each time you exhale, repeat a word or a phrase that is meaningful to you. Disregarding the everyday thoughts that come to your mind, return to your repetition and your breathing for ten to fifteen minutes. Once you finish, remain seated and quiet, allowing your thoughts to continue, then open your eyes and sit another minute or two before standing up.

Medical researchers are exploring demonstrable changes in brainwave patterns during meditation, but many people believe that by using the Relaxation Response they start and finish their day in a more tranquil state. Gradually, stressful situations will be less so; your sense of equanimity, joyfulness, optimism, and self-esteem will be enhanced.

It is difficult to achieve serenity if your child is running from a sports practice to a music or other lesson and then home to do homework and chores each day. Avoid over-scheduling your children. Don't overcrowd a child's week, even though you can afford to pay for many activities.

Unstructured play time opens the mind to thinking creatively, discovering new ideas, and learning to prob-lem solve. It also provides a relaxed and tranquil time for parent-child interaction. Resist the temptation to crowd a child's schedule with sports, tutoring, or various lessons. Overscheduling often leads to stressed out, mentally and physically exhausted children, and sometimes leads to a drop in school grades. Eventually, your child will become anxious, overtired, or irritable and possibly all three. Even middle and high school students need some unstructured time to explore various interests. Let them discover their own challenges and enjoy them at their own pace.

Ask your child what they really want to do; watch which activities they look forward to and which they attend with reluctance. Give your children plenty of free time when school is not in session. Children need to learn to entertain themselves. Summertime can be valuable emotionally and contribute to a child's intel-lectual development, creativity, and ability to deepen friendships. Don't let your children feel that they are always following someone else's script. Allow them to feel they are the authors of their own lives.

VIRTUE 4
Hard Work and Thrift

AS OUR SON grew older, his chores grew from putting away his toys, to helping take out the trash. Then, setting the dinner table and clearing off the dirty dishes and loading the dishwasher were added to his chores. It required a lot of parental serenity to not react if a few were dropped and broken in the process. The lessons learned were more important than any glass or plate; however, as he grew older and knew the value of the crockery, he paid for a broken item from his allowance and fewer were broken.

CHARACTERISTICS OF THESE TRAITS. Implant in your children habits of industry and thrift, and you lay the foundation for a life of achievement. The more disciplined they are, the more opportunities will exist for them.

TECHNIQUES TO BUILD WORK ETHIC AND THRIFT. To build work ethic, start small. Training a child to do tasks accurately and without delay will prepare him or her to do far bigger things carefully and promptly as an adult.

Even during the dependent stage of development (up to age ten), a child ought to be initiated in responsibility. He or she must have duties and perform them daily. You don't want to produce a dependent and helpless child like the ten-year-old who recently stayed at our home for a weekend. At breakfast he demanded toast and became quite irate when told where he could find the bread and the toaster. To our amazement, he responded: "I don't know how to make toast myself, it is always made for me."

Give each child increasing responsibilities. First, these duties may seem rather insignificant, such as keeping toys in order. The performance of duties of ever increasing significance prepares children for performing the greater tasks life will present to them as adults. It is also about each member making a contribution to the family. It is an important lesson because the family depends on each member fulfilling his or her responsibilities. Children trained in punctuality, in effort, in concentration, will, as adults, find responsibility a delight and constructive action a pleasure.

Emphasize academic responsibility over grades or awards. A responsible student: attends school every day (unless sick); follows directions; asks questions; works independently or cooperates on a team project; diligently prepares homework each day; and sets aside review time before an exam. By eliminating any judgmental factor based on grades, each child will feel good about being a learner. Acknowledge their responsible behavior and provide encouragement for their efforts and improvement at school. If you expect your children to place a high priority on education, don't take them away from school regularly for extended periods of time. Otherwise, you communicate that other things are more important than school.

Even elementary school-aged children need to learn to set priorities, focus their energies, and do tasks in order of importance. This is a valuable lesson, especially for the multi-tasking, overcommitted children and adults of today's world.

Emphasize the desirability of perseverance, of "hanging in there," in the midst of difficulties. Demonstrate to your children that they can find a way around life's challenges and obstacles without being overwhelmed or defeated.

Learning perseverance by taking a project from start to finish is important. For example, lead a child through the steps of gardening from planting seeds, watering them, and watching them sprout. This simple project gives youngsters practice in starting a project and seeing it through to completion. They also learn that if some of the seeds fail to grow, they must try again. Children who persist in gardening without giving up as adults generally are not quitters.

Build work ethic between ages five and ten. This is when children love to accomplish things; it is time to foster the good feelings that come from accomplishment. Celebrate tasks attempted and those completed with positive words, without overdoing it. Saying "good job" for absolutely everything makes it a meaningless and somewhat annoying phrase.

By connecting work with earning money, a child develops sound work habits and discipline. Those who start earlier have an easier time acquiring these traits than children who do not work for pay until after college.

Much has been written about the value of "McJobs," routine menial fast-food restaurant work. We believe that a paid work experience during teen years is invaluable. Work enables children to enjoy the satisfaction of achievement without parental involvement. Work experiences provide privileged youth with an understanding of and an appreciation for those who toil at low-level tasks. It gives them exposure to the realities of the world. Encourage your teen to take a part-time or summer job that is mundane, even boring, such as in a fast-food restaurant. It is important for teens to "suit up and show up" on time every day as expected, get along with coworkers and customers, and see the need for and the challenge of trying to make something more out of their lives. A part-time job caddying at the country club for parents and their friends may not have the same impact as going through the application and hiring process as an unknown prospect.

A part-time or summer job is important because teens learn responsibility and gain a sense of competence and achievement. But don't be too controlling as to the choice of employment. A child doesn't have to do the same thing you did to build character. If your child wants to do regularly scheduled volunteer work for a particular cause, encourage that goal. Furthermore, keep part-time work during the school year within reasonable bounds, generally not more than fifteen hours a week, so your teen doesn't disengage from school. Cut back on the hours if grades suffer and limit the weekday evening hours.

Social leveling occurs when a college-bound child gets a taste of work life. Children of privilege ought not to grow up believing they are "too good" for certain kinds of work. After your teen spends the summer flipping hamburgers and stuffing bags with fries, he or she will also likely strive to do better academically so that he or she will never do that kind of work in the future. If a child doesn't like fast-food restaurants, let him or her select something different.

A work ethic is desirable, but not all of your children will have your desire for achievement. Let go of certain expectations. Your child's talents and dreams may be counter to what you want for him or her. *Remember:* Children are blessed with different gifts, interests, and passions. To stimulate your child's drive, help him or her discover his or her passions. Allow each to define their own passions, interests, and competencies and then create their own identities and part-time or summer jobs.

The daughter of close friends was told she needed glasses at age fourteen. She insisted on designer frames, but frequently lost her glasses or broke them beyond repair. After replacing the three or four lost pairs of glasses, her affluent parents decided she would have to pay for all future replacements. She soon purchased less expensive frames and eventually stopped losing her glasses.

A WORD OR two on the subject of thrift. If you train your children to be frugal, it is unlikely that they will become adult hyperconsumers. Before buying something, teach each to ask: "Do I really need it? Can I wait a week to buy it? Can I do without it altogether? Do I own anything that I could substitute for it?"

Begin small to impart thrift. Teach your children to always turn out the lights when they leave a room. Tell them you pay for the electricity you use each month. Even though you have the money, it's a matter of priorities. Do they want the cash to go to the electric company or for pizza after school or on Sunday night?

The subject of thrift quickly goes into the more general subject of financial management. Thus, the topics of cash allowances and credit cards for children will be discussed in Chapter 6.

4 Three Interpersonal Character Traits: Lovingkindness, Forgiveness, Integrity

This chapter considers three key interpersonal character traits: lovingkindness, forgiveness, and integrity. Again, after briefly discussing the characteristics of each trait, practical techniques to build these traits are presented.

VIRTUE 5
Lovingkindness

A NINE-YEAR-OLD GIRL, whose main source of pride was her beautiful head of long blonde curly hair, developed cancer and had to undergo chemotherapy. She returned from a course of treatment completely bald and horribly ashamed of it. Her seven-year-old brother laughed at her and teased her mercilessly as she walked into their home. She burst into tears.

Her mother quietly took her to her bedroom and just held her, cuddling and soothing her with whispers of reassurance. While the initial incident took only a few minutes, the little girl took months to recover from her brother's laughter. What sustained her was her mother's quiet cuddling and reassurances.

CHARACTERISTICS OF THIS TRAIT. Love is the power that makes for harmony and happiness. It brings people together and holds the world together. Love heals and soothes. Love represents a giving to and a sharing with others. It enables us to experience the world from another's perspective. At the heart of love is the choice to live by compassion and kindness. These attributes help link us to others.

Compassion is a matter of feeling with and for others. Opening one's heart to others' pain and suffering enables each of us to experience our unity with others. It helps us understand how connected we all are. Compassion also implies a tender interpretation of others' motives, words, and deeds.

Kindness represents compassion in action. Do not let bitterness, anger, or indifference cloud the natural kindness in your heart.

People who show lovingkindness to others are cherished. They provide examples for the rest of us to follow.

TECHNIQUES TO BUILD LOVINGKINDNESS. By planting in your children the habit of lovingkindness toward others, you prepare them to be desirable members of humanity.

Teach your children to express their inherent love of compassion and kindness to others. Strive to instill in them lessons of love, compassion, and kindness. Ask your children to put themselves in the place of others, to identify with others, to do for others what they expect others to do for them. Draw forth the inherent potentiality for lovingkindness so that it becomes a habit for each of them.

In the wake of the Columbine High School and other school-based horrors, much has been written about school bullies. Many of these bullies are found to come from homes where there is an absence of lovingkindness, whether because of divorce, alcohol, drugs, or other issues.

In teaching your children to express lovingkindness in words and deeds, begin by demonstrating these traits yourself and then seek compassion and kindness from your children. Develop the expectation that your children will perform acts of compassion and speak words of kindness. One compassionate deed, one kind word will spark your children to perform another compassionate act and speak another kind word.

Due to an early childhood illness, seven-year-old Robby was the smallest child in his second grade class. Yet, this very small boy had a big heart. Early one day, while playing in the school yard with the other boys, a father appeared with his eight-year-old son, who was unusually large for his age. The new student was in tears and clung to his father, pleading not to be left at the new school. Without a single word, tiny Robby walked over to the crying boy, took his hand and pulled him with all his small might toward the play area where other boys were watching, and without a word threw him their ball, engaging him in their game. The stunned father quietly made his escape but he never forgot that wordless kindness. The two boys grew up to become best friends through their school years together and later, despite having lived in different countries, Robby was the best man at his friend's wedding. The parents of both boys learned from that little boy's gesture that compassionate and loving actions may be dramatic and even more powerful than words.

Let your children see your compassion and kindness in action. Nothing binds one to another more closely than a compassionate word or a kind act. Let your words and acts demonstrate your lovingkindness. Try to extend your love to everyone by daily performing small acts of compassion and kindness, building one upon another.

Let your children see how you practice love throughout the day. Express your love in every situation by doing and speaking the good and the beautiful.

Try to be a love finder, not a fault finder. Do not focus on what is wrong or lacking in others. Being a love finder means opening your heart and mind to the wonders you see around you. There is something positive in everyone, even in seemingly "difficult" people. Strive to see the goodness in others.

Begin each day with thoughts of compassion and kindness for others. Express your lovingkindness in your deeds. Train your tongue to speak kind words. Try to minimize (and hopefully eliminate) negative talk about others. Speak words that encourage, that bring out the best in others, that inspire others to higher achievements.

Let your deeds demonstrate your lovingkindness. Strive to generate goodwill between yourself and others as well as among people. Through your conduct, be a helper to all and an enemy to none. Extend hospitality to others. Bring peace between people. As you do something each day to make others feel better, your children will learn from you by example.

Theresa was the office manager in a law firm, supervising about a dozen administrative assistants. One Friday afternoon one of the junior attorneys submitted a large work order that absolutely had to be done within the next 36 hours so he could take the work with him on a trip to present it to a client. Theresa informed six of her assistants that they would have to stay very late on Friday evening and work most of Saturday to get the work done. There was a great deal of grumbling and complaining because, despite a generous overtime and Saturday cash bonus, they all had to cancel various weekend social plans. After much cajoling and a generous ordering of food, the work was done. Theresa arrived early on Sunday morning to make sure that the senior partner and his junior attorney had all their necessary documents ready to go. When the senior partner saw what had been done he was horrified and ordered her to delete 90 percent of the work the assistants had just finished on Saturday. Theresa never told her assistants that their personal lives had been disrupted for no good reason, but on Monday morning rewarded them appropriately and thanked them profusely for their willingness to complete the project on time. The only ones she told were her husband and children.

By speaking kind words and performing acts of compassion, the habit of lovingkindness will become the deepest part of your children's being. As they fill their hearts with love for everyone, implementing these feelings through their words and deeds, others will respond with love. The more your children love, the more they will be loved.

However, remind your children that sometimes the lovingkindness they express may not be returned. You and your children should love without any expectation of another's positive response. One's lovingkindness ought to be unconditional and selfless.

Direct the character trait of lovingkindness to others into altruistic channels. Let lovingkindness find its expression in deeds—in doing for others. Love that expresses itself in service to others grows ever stronger and deeper with each act of service performed. At an appropriate age, teach each of your children the habit of charity.

Set an example. Each day strive to express your love through selfless service to others. Ask yourself: what can you best do for others to help relieve their pain and suffering and to aid them in experiencing happiness and developing hopefulness?

These acts of lovingkindness need not be on a grand scale. You can assist others with your humor, your counsel and advice, your talents, or your money. Give of yourself to others through whatever means is appropriate to you. Consider volunteering in your community. Your children will see how you serve others locally.

At about age five, you can begin to make each of your children aware that most people are not rich. Remind them that the privileged have a duty to try to help those less fortunate in meaningful, constructive ways, but not to see them as victims.

Talk about those children who are less fortunate, some of whom go to bed hungry. These conversations will help your youngsters begin to understand how privileged they are. It likely will lead to their thinking about how to help by sharing their good fortune with others. Even a young child can give toys or clothes to someone less fortunate. Bringing him or her with you when you give these away so he or she feels part of the process is more potent than just delivering them yourself.

Asking your child to select one or two toys he or she no longer wants and bringing your child with you to a charitable organization makes a lasting impression on a youngster. There is little doubt that a child learns more about lovingkindness and charity from participating in these activities than in watching his or her parents write a check and mail it off.

A ten-year-old can learn lovingkindness by doing good deeds. Demonstrate the power of personal involvement through your volunteering at your child's school or offering your help in the local community. These demonstrate a charitable mindset on your part. Talk to your ten or twelve-year-old about the volunteer activities that you are involved in. For instance, share the challenge of meeting an organization's fundraising or some other goal. Your actions speak louder than your words. Make the topic familiar to your children. Answer any questions they pose with an informational, but short, answer.

Strive to find a way to make a difference in the world, even on a small scale, with each child, especially one who is cynical. Try to involve him or her with something greater than him- or herself.

Begin by volunteering together, as a family, or at least one parent and a child, on a weekend afternoon project so that volunteering becomes a way of life. But don't drag your youngster into a volunteer situation. Volunteer where your child has a passion or an interest even if it is not yours. Participate with your child by working side by side; start with an activity that requires involvement once or twice a month. Talk with your child about the activity after you both participate. Praise him or her for doing a good deed. Going to a nursing home or hospice may be too strange and uncomfortable for a younger child. Try going to an animal shelter, a school for severely disabled children, or a youth-oriented program.

As discussed in Chapter 6, impart the key lessons in giving by starting early, empowering each of your children by letting them choose what to give from their allowances and to whom. Ralph lived comfortably with his mother, Edith. While Ralph was still an infant, his father died a few days before Christmas. Each year, on the anniversary of his father's death, Ralph gave a donation to a family with children but no father in the home. At first this was just a few dollars from his allowance, but as he grew older his donations increased accordingly.

Let each explain to you what organizations they want to give money to and his or her reasons for selecting these organizations. Charitable behavior, giving from one's heart and not out of a sense of guilt, is learned behavior and must be molded and reinforced. Consider requiring your children to contribute a part, say 10 percent, of their allowance to charity. Choose a percentage or an amount with which you and they are comfortable.

Initiating a dialogue about charitable giving introduces the idea to your children that they are fortunate and with money comes a responsibility to share some of that wealth with others. It helps children understand the realities of the world, but doesn't make them feel guilty about how much they have. Through communication and collaboration you build charitable attitudes that last a lifetime: the expectation that your children will do something meaningful with any money you give them or that they will inherit from you.

Over many years of college teaching, we have observed that privileged students who go to Florida beaches for spring break do not return to class as refreshed and invigorated as those who went to New Orleans to help rebuild after Katrina or other such projects. Children who feel that they are making a difference, whether through volunteering or charitable giving or both, become more grounded, self-confident adults, having a sense of community and connectedness to others. Charitable endeavors help them develop a sense of purpose in life and build the character trait of lovingkindness.

Train a child to direct his or her compassion and kindness to others, so that he or she does not spend it on him or herself. You do not want any of your offspring to see the world and humanity as existing only for his or her sake. This narcissistic interpretation of lovingkindness—which should be a noble character trait—makes an individual obnoxious to others and may render him or her incapable of experiencing happiness.

VIRTUE 6
Forgiveness

"Forgiving is not forgetting, it's letting go of the hurt."
–Mary McLeod Bethune

CHARACTERISTICS OF THIS TRAIT. Love and forgiveness are interrelated. You experience love by extending forgiveness to others. By forgiving others, you open your heart and rediscover the capacity to love.

Forgiveness is love in action. Forgiveness sets us free to love and create new relationships with old enemies. By letting go of the past, we are able to embrace a creative future in which old wounds become the basis for a new beginning. However, forgiveness does not imply that we allow others to continue to abuse, manipulate, or oppress us.

You experience love by extending forgiveness to others, by accepting others, and by letting go of the past. By forgiving, you invite love to replace hatred, resentment, fear, anger, rejection, blame, or disappointment, any of which constrict one's heart and narrow one's world.

Forgiveness also represents a key to cultivating serenity—one's inner peace of mind (Virtue 3). Forgiveness helps leave behind past, often painful, experiences that otherwise continue to allow the offender to maintain control over you. In short, forgiveness not only absolves someone else—the perpetrator—it also heals you, the victim.

TECHNIQUES TO BUILD FORGIVENESS. Forgiveness is not easy. It is hard to forgive, particularly if you have been hurt badly by a major breach of trust.

As you demonstrate forgiveness to your children, recognize that it often demands courage and a strong sense of self (Virtue 1) to overcome the pain you have experienced. Your child has just spilled grape juice on your new living room carpeting. Take a deep breath before you do anything else!

Start with something small—perhaps something that impacted you and one of your children. Think of striving to choose forgiveness in the face of being tempted to see another's rather thoughtless deeds or harmful words as a personal attack on you and to respond, in turn, with your own counterattack. In forgiving others, you cannot pretend that you were not affected by someone's hurtful conduct or speech. Forgiving is not permissiveness. By forgiving, you do not pronounce as acceptable someone's cruelty, thoughtlessness, or dishonesty. It does not mean condoning, accepting, or justifying another's actions or statements. How would you feel if you had committed the wrong? Would you want forgiveness?

Through forgiveness you come to accept those who have disappointed you by not being perfect. By judging others less severely, you become more accepting of human frailty. You demonstrate to your children that you are willing to let go of your focus on another's "guilt," not hold on to the past, and not let your anger and hate continue to poison you. Relinquishing your thought of retribution lifts the self-defeating weight of anger and hate from your shoulders.

Let your children see how you shift your perspective and strive to see things differently through forgiveness. This shift in perception helps dissolve your hate, restore your inner peace of mind, and reduce both your anxiety and unhealthy anger.

A woman who had once cheated during her marriage created a strong resentment in her husband. He in turn went out and had a short-lived sexual affair to get even. Each actually loved the other and didn't care about the person with whom they had the affair. The man hurt himself in his revenge far more than his wife, who understood his anger. Their children were old enough to sense much of what happened and were hurt for years afterward.

As discussed in connection with the virtue of equanimity (Virtue 3), reframing a situation facilitates your understanding of an event and someone else. Seeing another in the light of love may help you to perceive another's true essence, his or her essential innocence and worth, deserving of your lovingkindness.

Although it seems difficult, realize that many times others' hurtful deeds and words may deep down be a plea for love. As another cries out, try to meet their cries as an expression of a desire to be healed and loved, not attacked or judged harshly. Teach your children that each of us has the same need and longing for love and inner peace of mind. By seeing others through the eyes of lovingkindness and forgiveness, not with the mindset of judgment, punishment, or moral superiority, you are able to answer another's acts or words with love, letting go of the rest— your fears, hatred, or anger.

Teach your children that forgiveness begins with self-forgiveness. Demonstrate the need to overcome any lingering beliefs as to your unworthiness. By letting go of your feelings of self-doubt and building your self-esteem (Virtue 1), you give others the ability to make mistakes.

There is no magic formula to put forgiveness into practice. Start by acknowledging the hurt, recognizing that someone did something harmful to you. Then decide to forgive, seeing another through the eyes of love, not through the eyes of judgment or guilt. Through a shift in perception, try to receive a new vision of the other person, helping replace the pain with an inner peace of mind. But remember that forgiving means saying "no more," this time from a calm, quiet place. Do not condone another's hurtful deeds or words. If you anticipate an ongoing relationship, set some boundaries on future interactions.

If your heart does not allow you to love someone you have forgiven, try to think of some great goodness in him or her. Strive to find one good quality or hope for something good for that person so that you may come to better perceive his or her inner worth, however difficult it may be.

"I'm sorry" is one of the most difficult phrases to say to someone and to mean, but the words are powerful to receive. This is true in both personal and business relationships. When a major Fortune 500 corporation discovered it had caused many of its employees to be permanently injured and even had caused numerous deaths from air pollution in one of its factories, it offered to make cash settlements to the employees' families. To the surprise of the attorneys in charge of the settlement conferences, what the widows and children of the former employees wanted more than cash or anything else was for someone from management to face them and say "I'm sorry" for the harm done to their loved ones.

If you have hurt someone, take the initiative and say, "I'm sorry." Making amends will help you as much as the person you are apologizing to. These two little words will help the two of you move forward and may be the most valuable thing you can do to right a wrong.

VIRTUE 7
Integrity

CHARACTERISTICS OF THIS TRAIT. Truthfulness and honesty are the hallmarks of integrity. Along with lovingkindness and forgiveness, these traits serve as the foundation on which interpersonal relationships are based. Truthfulness and honesty represent a key to one's character and one's dealings with others. Someone truthful and honest is an ideal individual, one who is trusted without reservation.

TECHNIQUES TO BUILD INTEGRITY. When our son was about ten years old, he received a check from his ailing grandfather to buy a game of his choice. He was taken to a large toy store for that purpose, selected the deluxe version of a favorite and paid for it at the cashier. As we got into the car and discussed his purchase, I (his mother) realized that he had been charged the price for the basic model but had received the deluxe edition. I asked him what he thought they should do about this situation. He stared at me as though I had lost my mind, but after a long moment of silence he decided we should return to the store and correct the problem. It was his choice whether he would pay the additional amount for the deluxe model or whether he could be satisfied with the basic version. He recalled that event for many years thereafter.

Train your children to be truthful and honest with themselves and with others. Let your children see your striving to live out who and what you are. It is not easy to stop deceiving yourself and others and admit your false-hoods. Say what you mean and mean what you say. A "Yes" should mean yes; a "No" should mean no.

Begin by being truthful and honest with yourself, so that you can be truthful and honest with others. Do not blame others for your shortcomings or misdoings. Ac-knowledge your own deficiencies and strive to correct them. Let your children see and understand this.

After the age where the realities of Santa Claus and the Tooth Fairy are accepted, do not deceive others, including your children. Don't tell your spouse to tell someone on the telephone that you are not at home when you lack the courage to speak to that individual. Your children are listening and will remember that event. Let truthfulness and honesty become key principles in every one of your relationships with others. By telling people the truth and acting honestly, others will come to trust and respect you. Strive to place truth and honesty at the center of your existence.

This does not mean hurtful honesty. We don't mean to suggest telling your friend she looks fat in a certain dress, but you don't have to compliment her on an unflattering outfit either.

Teach your children by example. Show them that life is far richer and more pleasant with a healthy conscience and a little less wealth than with a troubled conscience and more money. Emphasize the importance of truthfulness and honesty in all of your children's dealings with others, starting with you, your spouse, their siblings, and their friends.

5 Dealing with Outside Influences and Their Impact on Character Development

E ven if you provide the best home environment, outside influences impact on your children's development. This chapter considers two of these influences: a child's school and his or her friends. It concludes with the impact of other influences—television and the Internet—on character development.

Selecting a School

THERE IS NOTHING more valuable to your child's future than a solid educational and behavioral foundation. Find a school, whether public or private, with sound academics, one that reinforces the positive character traits you wish to implant. Seek out a school that discovers a child's gifts, makes them productive, and finds an outlet for his or her best contributions. Search for a school that teaches students to build on their strengths and to look outside themselves for strengths that they will never possess. In addition to building a child's intellectual capital, a school should cultivate each youngster's potential and promote the appreciation of using one's talents and passions to contribute to broader goals beyond oneself.

Remember: The decisions you make at each step of a child's educational career offer no foolproof guarantees of success. Even the "best" private schools do not suit the needs of all children.

You must decide whether to go the private or public school route. Typically, classes at private schools are significantly smaller than public counterparts, even in the best neighborhoods. Better student-to-teacher ratios help ensure that the adults are more likely to know each child. But there are other factors, including facilities, extracurricular programs, range of subjects and advanced courses offered, opportunities for a child with a learning disability, diversity, both economic and racial, of the student body, and community outreach programs. Most important, perhaps, you want to select a school, whether public or private, where the children come from families that value education and character development above material possessions. Check the parent-teacher association for its activities and how many of the parents participate in its activities. Whatever you choose, don't let your child get bored in class or be bullied by peers, whether person-to-person or online (so-called "cyberbullying").

Your Child's Friends

MARK WAS FROM a middle-class Jewish family and attended an extremely diverse school. He developed a close friendship with a Middle Eastern boy from an ultra-wealthy family. Mark's parents were cautiously pleased with this friendship, but more concerned about the financial dispar-ity than the cultural or religious differences. All was well until one Halloween when Mark's mother surreptitiously followed the boys in their trick-or-treat adventure. While Mark played a few harmless pranks, the other boy did cruel and destructive things to people's pets, flower beds, and other property. Upon closer examination, Mark's mother discovered that this friend had very little adult supervi-sion and seemed to do as he pleased, with a very generous allowance supporting his every desire. Unfortunately, he seemed to crave parental attention, which was the one thing really missing from his privileged life.

Learn how and with whom your children spend their time. Parents usually think (or fear) the worst, but gen-erally are pleasantly surprised. To be able to make your own judgment, ascertain the friends with whom your children associate inside and outside of school. Don't be too overt in your investigative activities. To see that the company your child keeps is constructive, chaperone a school event, go camping with your child, their friends, and the friends' parents, or get involved in a volunteer effort at your child's school.

It is not enough to simply ask "What do your friend's parents do for a living?" and "Where do they live?" as one of our acquaintances did. Making judgments about their financial resources does not tell you about their value sys-tem and how they are raising their children. To this day, this father has no idea of some of his daughter's wild ad-ventures with her friends.

Train your children to cultivate friends of good char-acter, so that they will learn from their words and deeds. Help them spend time with friends who demonstrate positive character traits. Conversely, train your children to avoid peers of bad character so that they are less likely to engage in self-destructive behavior, including substance abuse, unplanned pregnancy, viewing of Internet pornography, neglecting studies, or eating disorders. Bad companions may exert an even stronger influence on your children than you do as a parent. If a child's peers dwell on superficial things, such as weight or physical appearance, suggest changing friends. Also, encourage your children to make friends with older individuals, to gain a broader perspective on life and events.

Remember: Let your children concentrate on goals they can control, with whom and how they spend their time, and focus on developing their own interests and talents.

Amelia came from an upper-middle-class, professional family with a great deal of education and financial resources. Caroline, her best friend for her last three years of high school, was from a different religion and economic class, and had parents who had not had much formal education. From this relationship, Amelia learned the value of knowing people for their personal attributes, not for their education or monetary assets.

It is important for your privileged children to have friends from diverse socioeconomic backgrounds. Friendships outside your socioeconomic group allow a child to gain a larger view of the world. To enable them to function successfully with all types of people and prevent their world from being too narrow, encourage all types of positive friendships for your children. They will have to interact with all sorts of people when they are adults.

Remember: Never look down on others who are not wealthy; otherwise, you will likely cut your children off from much of the world. Don't make derogatory remarks about less-affluent people. Critique generalizations about group members. Teach your children that wealth does not make some people better or worse than others.

The teen years are especially important, but often difficult for both you as a parent and your child. A teen's peers often become a child's collective parents. If you don't have a good relationship with your teenager, he or she may seek out peers or a friend's parents. This will only create jealousy and possibly anger in you, widening the chasm between you and your teen. It may be difficult, but your teenager needs you even when he or she seems to be pushing you away.

Dave's parents lost the bond with their teenage son. He spent so much time at his friend's home that the friend's mother knew when Dave had his first date with a girl, where they went, and when they shared their first kiss. Dave's mother never knew details. She only knew if she wanted to find her son, she could call Dave's friend's house and someone would know where he was. She maintained a jealous attitude toward the friend's mother for years after both boys went off to college.

Teens generally desire to be part of a group yet be unique in some ways. It is important to get to know your child's friends and your teen's dating practices. Spending time with a group of risk-taking friends is hazardous for any teenager, particularly in an unsupervised setting.

Encourage your teen to join different groups to meet new people. As a last resort, forbid association with certain friends. This last action should be used cautiously, as making certain people "off limits" may make them more appealing.

As discussed in Chapter 1, a regular family hour is important. Surveys show that teens who regularly eat dinner with their parents are better students and are less likely to smoke, drink, or use illicit drugs. The family dinner hour is a great time to learn about the character of your child's friends.

Other Influences

FROM DOWNLOADING, TEXT messaging, YouTube, Facebook, MySpace and the whole range of electronic access to the world, a child faces many temptations for which they may be too immature.

Teach your children to avoid magazines, films, TV programs, and Internet sites that emphasize superficialities over good character and behavior. Be a role model for your youngsters.

By providing many enticing and deleterious influences, television and the Internet pose special problems. For instance, manufacturers use television to turn children into toy-hungry seekers, destined to nag parents into buying the latest toy, which will occupy them for all of thirty minutes. Monitor how much television your children watch, especially commercials for toys and other nonessentials. At an early age, get them in the habit of moving away from the TV when commercials begin, to physically move their bodies and eyes away from the screen.

Again, be a role model. The amount and kind of television your offspring are exposed to often depends on the amount and kind of viewing you do.

Carefully limit television viewing. Perhaps tie the amount of television time to other activities, such as a half hour of TV viewing for a half hour of walking with you.

Keep the computer out of your child's bedroom and place it in a den, living room, or other area where you can see what the child is viewing. Supervise each of your children's Internet use. Put time limits on your children's Web use. Consider a Web filter to help you control what they see and do online, at least at home. It is impossible to block all the sites that already exist and that are being added every day, but parents should be vigilant. Parental control software lets you filter out objectionable content and block sites of your choosing.

Check in and ask your child to show you his Web pages, profiles, and blogs. Set firm Web rules, including: 1) needing parental permission before entering personal information into a Web site; 2) not answering an e-mail or a text message from a stranger; and 3) not showing information on a social networking site that makes it easy for a stranger to find him or her, thereby avoiding an easy prey for a kidnapper or molester. Never let your child give out a cell phone number to someone he or she doesn't already know. Also, supervise the selection and use of video games.

In short, control and monitor what your children do with home computers, on- and offline. If you can, randomly check their Web site contact history after they have gone to bed. Being informed and vigilant is critical in this digital society, but your job will be easier if you teach your child to be vigilant for themselves.

PART II

How to Protect Your Wealth from Being
Destroyed by Your Children and Grandchildren

6 Money Matters and Character Development: How to Raise Financially Fit Children

You worked hard, saved, and invested wisely and now have a sizable estate. Do you want your heirs to dissipate it all in a big spending spree?

You need to train your children in the competencies they will eventually need to make decisions when they receive your wealth. Otherwise, your financial assets may be at risk from uninformed and incompetent inheritors. The greatest risk to your financial assets may be from your children (and grandchildren), not the legal strategies you implement or the investment management techniques you adopt.

Affluent families seldom discuss monetary limitations. Children see that material possessions continually appear, rather magically; the supply of money appears endless. Many offspring grow up naïve about financial responsibility. They are often financially reckless and look to their parents to bail them out. But pretending not to have money creates problems as well. Wealthy parents shouldn't pretend to be middle-class.

Do not expect every one of your children to become a financial wizard. Hopefully, one of your children will develop the competency necessary to assume leadership in this area and become the trusted financial resource for the next generation. However, all family members need to be responsible for learning basic financial concepts. Even if a child never develops much facility with finance, he or she should learn the big picture and feel comfortable raising questions and discussing financial matters with your (and later, their) advisors.

Talking About Money with Your Children

NOT EVERY FIVE-YEAR-OLD can be like the one we overheard in a bank one day. When asked by a teller if he could write his name, he quickly responded: "Of course I can. How else could I endorse a check?"

Overcome the money taboo. Talk openly with your children about money. Many wealthy parents are uncomfortable doing it because they were raised by parents who felt uncomfortable talking to them about money. Don't follow their lead.

Tell children the truth as is age-appropriate, but don't lecture. Build a child's trust in you by helping him or her make sense of family wealth. It will build his or her confidence that there are no family secrets. Talking to your children about money shows that you respect them. Conversely, withholding information conveys a lack of trust, leaving a void for imagination to take hold in ways you would not expect or appreciate. A child who learns too little or nothing at all will likely use his or her imagination or the Internet to fill in the blanks. Family secrecy may lead a child to infer that the topic is shameful; he or she may grow up uncomfortable about money and about him or herself as a wealth inheritor. He or she may feel betrayed, especially if you always tell him or her you can't afford things, and may not acquire the skills needed to manage money. The risk of dampening a child's motivation to go to (or finish) college or cultivate a satisfying career may be greater if you hide the truth for years, and then suddenly spring it on a twenty-one-year-old, who lacks the opportunity to prepare for it or integrate it into his or her values and goals.

A child's age and maturity enter into the picture. At age five or eight, it's easy for parents to shield their children from realizing the family has more money, often much more than others. Even then discuss with them, perhaps at Thanksgiving, that the family is blessed with many things—good health, a nice place to live, freedom from worrying about paying for food. Emphasize your gratefulness for the financial security that makes this abundance possible.

One ultra-wealthy father had flown his family on a private jet for their vacation. When it came time to return their rental car, the father made a point of teaching his three children to save the valet fee and return the car with him. The lesson was an important one, but also very expensive since the jet engines were already burning fuel while waiting for the family.

Even with an eight-year-old who cannot comprehend vast sums of money, share a story about how your father (or grandfather) founded a company that helped family members. Children are fascinated with the past; it puts wealth in a context they can understand.

Talk about the family legacy: who made the money and how? If you inherited wealth, convey the qualities of its generators. Children may be less likely to squander family money if they realize that generations have worked hard to earn it.

If affluence is new to your family, talk about your life before and after you became wealthy. Emphasize the importance of vision, risktaking, and hard work. Even if wealth did not come as a result of your effort, begin to develop that it means for good health care, educational opportunities, and more options.

For those of more modest income, an excellent method is what Nancy did with her four children. She gathered them around a table and put a pile of Monopoly money equal to their monthly net income in the middle. Then she gave each child a real bill and told the child to take the necessary amount to pay the bill. As the pile dwindled from payments for telephone, electricity, and other necessities, the children quickly understood why they couldn't indulge their every whim.

By age ten, a child of a wealthy family may read about the family's net worth in the newspaper, see it on the Internet, or hear about it from a friend on a school bus. Corporate filings with the Securities and Exchange Commission provide more detail than ever before on compensation and generous compensation packages appear on the front page of some newspapers and in magazines. Web sites enable a curious youngster to calculate the value of family houses.

When your ten-year-old son asks, "How much money do you make," answer, "Enough for everything we need."

Because they generally lack a grasp of figures, don't tell children of this age exactly how much you make. You are entitled to your privacy.

When your eleven-year-old daughter asks, "Are we rich?" don't flat-out lie (remember Virtue 7) or be too vague. Rather, reply, "We are wealthier than many but not as wealthy as others in the neighborhood" (perhaps picking out a billionaire in the news). Emphasize, however, that compared to many others in the world, you are very well off, noting, "We have the resources to do many things, but also the obligation to help others who do not have your resources." You may want to add, "Let's not exaggerate the importance of money. Money as a means of keeping score is waste of one's time; it reflects badly on the kind of person you are." Remind her that your wealth does not make her better or worse than her peers. Tell her the money is not hers; it is yours. If she persists, asking, "Will I inherit the money?" tell her, "We will fund your education and perhaps help you buy a house or start a business. However, you will need to work hard and have you own career."

You may wonder: How can I help my daughter so that she will not alienate other kids by gloating obnoxiously about money? Or, what if you overhear your son bragging to his friends about the big house he lives in and comparing it to the value of their homes? Admonish him afterward; point out that he acted like a snob, that bragging is ugly, and firmly remind him: "This is my house and I worked hard for it."

Through your words and deeds, emphasize that arrogance and snobbery are bad character traits. Talk to your children about money, especially family money and the obligations that go with it. Encourage them to think about what money means. Does money mean power, a means to reduce guilt, a sign of personal success? Is it an end in itself for its own sake or a vehicle for achieving important things in life? Connect the concept of money with that of responsibility, on your part and that of your children.

Be honest. Start frank discussions about money with your children when they are in their early teens. As your teen's maturity and capacity to understand increases, your chats ought to become more and more detailed. Provide increasing amounts of information over the years in a way that is appropriate for each child's age and maturity. But don't overload them with information they may not understand.

Beginning in their early teen years, talk openly with your children about your wealth and the duties that come with it. Try to tie your money to the concept of stewardship and the importance of philanthropic endeavors.

Focus your discussion about your goals concerning family wealth, rather than merely talking about the nature and extent of your fortune. Communicating the positive character traits, such as a work ethic (Virtue 4) and lovingkindness (Virtue 5), the latter through volunteering and charitable giving, that are associated with the acquisition and management of wealth is far more important than detailing exact numbers.

Help your children develop a comfort level about money through age-appropriate conversations at home. The specifics are generally best left to the late teen years (or even later depending on each child's maturity level).

Details you tell an older sibling will inevitably trickle down to your younger children. All you can do is explain to your older children that you have entrusted them with information that they should not share with anyone, and hope for the best.

Allowances

ALLOWANCES CAN HELP children with seemingly unlimited material resources begin to learn that money does not appear mysteriously. Sound financial parenting begins with an allowance, a fixed amount that children receive at regular intervals—weekly for young children and usually monthly for high school-aged children.

Allowances provide an opportunity to reinforce teachings about character traits and the uses of money. Allowances also enable you to teach your children about financial responsibility, adding on responsibility as age-appropriate. The training your children receive with their allowances provides a natural bridge to deal with the more sophisticated aspects of financial management.

Handling money requires hands-on experience. An allowance provides an excellent vehicle for education and conversation about how to save, keep track of spending, and build and live within a budget. Putting aside money for a specific goal helps impart the discipline of deferred gratification.

Get to know each of your children and how much responsibility he or she can handle at each stage of his or her development. Here are some age-appropriate suggestions, but try to keep things simple so you and each child can manage it.

What's an appropriate age to begin an allowance? Give an allowance once a child asks you to buy things for him or her. Begin with a toy and candy allowance when they are five or six. Around first grade, children see the bigger picture and understand that money allows you to do and buy things. They begin to understand that spending money involves choices and the need to put off purchases. Self-control and delayed gratification are important, but don't push delayed gratification or you risk squeezing spontaneity out of your children. Teach the need to defer gratification, but allow for some instant gratification at the same time.

As you begin an allowance, discuss what it is supposed to cover. Explain what a child can buy and what's barred. *Remember*: An allowance is a tool for teaching money management. Tell your daughter: "Use your allowance to practice how to spend and save wisely."

Most children become fascinated with money at age seven or eight. They can count change and understand the relationship between prices and the ability to pay for an item.

Starting at age seven or eight, children should be required to make their bed each morning, help set the dinner table, and clean up their toys every evening. But don't pay for these basic tasks—an allowance isn't a salary. We realize that this is controversial, but regular household chores should not be paid for, because a family is not a business. Obligations must be shared, and children ought to feel that they are contributing family members. Occasionally you may pay for a special project, such as cleaning out the attic, to teach the concept of earning money.

Don't pay for good grades, because school is a child's job. Don't let a child associate academic achievement with money. Don't give an allowance tied to behavior modification, such as improvement in any one of the virtues. Why? The motivation for character traits ought to be intrinsic.

The reward for delayed gratification should be something a child wants, not what you think he or she should want. To teach deferred gratification, the reward for completing a task (for instance, practicing the piano) need not be cash. Instead, help your child find music he or she will enjoy playing and buy it for him or her.

You go shopping with your nine-year-old son who sees a beautiful racing bicycle. He says, "Mom, I love this bike. Buy it for me." You respond, "No way. That bike costs $750." Your son answers: "It's not a big deal for you and Dad. You make tons of money. Last night I heard you say it will cost $750 to get the Lexus serviced. We can afford it and I want it." So you buy the bike, rationalizing that your kids deserve what your money can buy for them, although not wanting them to be spoiled brats either. You feel guilty about your decision and your need for your child's approval.

It would have been better not to give in to your son's pressure, and to answer, "We can afford to buy the bicycle, but we choose not to. We don't want to spoil you." You can also tell him that there is such a thing as too much, saying, "I'll put it on your birthday or holiday wish list." If your son receives a substantial allowance, shift the burden onto him, stating, "Why don't you save money to buy it yourself, and I'll match you one dollar for every dollar you save?" Once he knows that he needs to help contribute to the cost, he'll then likely ask for a far less expensive bike.

Explain to your children why it is not in their best, long-term interests to obtain every item the minute they want it. Children of affluent parents learn critical life lessons from waiting and saving to achieve goals.

Teach your children the difference between a need and a want. Your children will come to thank you. Besides keeping them out of financial trouble, it will help them learn to deal with frustration in other aspects of life. To counter your daughter's demands for another DVD, answer, "I believe you have enough things already. If you want another DVD, save your money and I'll be happy to drive you to the store." Your daughter will learn to set financial priorities.

As your children become older, insist that they do chores as uncompensated duties, part of the sharing of family responsibilities around the house, not linked to an allowance. To cut down on the complaining, rotate recurring chores each week, so that one child doesn't always do the same task. Even if you have household help, reserve some tasks, such as raking leaves or cleaning out the garage, for your older children. At ten- to twelve-years-old, hire a child for special projects, such as washing a family car, cleaning the basement or attic, planting a garden in the spring, or putting away lawn furniture in the fall. For these extra chores around the home, be realistic about the going rate. If you pay a lot for a small chore, your youngster may unrealistically expect the same amount (or even more) outside the home.

Develop a list of extra chores and don't keep it a secret. Your children ought to be aware that if they need extra funds, they can perform these special tasks.

For expensive items, such as a computer, in addition to offering to match whatever your child saves from an allowance, birthday and holiday money, and cash earned by doing extra chores around the house, encourage your ten- to twelve-year-old to work outside the home, walking a neighbor's dog or babysitting. Working increases a child's sense of competency and control over his or her life. It helps provide a sense of purpose.

Set consistent limits for your children. Begin with one limit at a time. If a child isn't picking up his or her toys, making the beds, or taking out the garbage, tell him or her that you'll impose a monetary fine every time you have to do the chore yourself. Once you get that under control, move on. *Remember*: Children respond to different things; for some, it may be money, for others, it may be restricting access to the television or the computer.

What is a reasonable amount for an allowance? Give an allowance in an amount that is somewhat less than a child says he or she needs. Rather than taking a wild stab at what seems like a realistic amount, talk with other parents in your child's class. See what they are giving and expecting in return, but don't be a slave to their norms. Or, as a rough rule of thumb, give one dollar for every year of age per week, so that an eight-year-old would receive $8 a week. Don't make it so low as to be unreasonable or so high that a child doesn't need to make spending choices.

To set a number, decide what it is designed to cover. Consider what a child actually needs and how much money he or she can comfortably handle. Work with a child to make a list of the basics and the fun stuff, attach realistic prices, and add it up. Start small and increase an allowance with a child's heightened sense of responsibility. Don't increase an allowance until a child masters the degree of financial responsibility commensurate with his or her age and developmental stage as well as the items the allowance is designed to cover.

Once a child has access to a computer, watch out. He or she can make noncash purchases, download music or online video games, or incur PayPal charges for eBay collectibles. To calculate an allowance, you likely will have to untangle a number of electronic transactions and find out which child is responsible for which charges. Apart from not giving any of your children your credit card information, their own credit (or debit) card, or devising your own charge-tracking spreadsheet, you may want to turn to allowance-tracking Web sites or special prepaid debit cards that you load up with money online and that e-mail you each time one of your children makes a charge.

Budgeting is a key financial skill. A child learns the value of money and the need to set priorities. He or she must manage the limited funds you provide. To teach this, sit down with a child and map out various weekly (or monthly) expenses. In trying to provide real-life conditions, set reasonable parameters. After a child masters the basics of budgeting, give them the responsibility of preparing a budget and presenting it to you. You and your child will likely have to compromise on some items. By showing that you respect him or her, he or she generally will rise to the occasion, becoming a responsible contributor to the budgeting process. If your child demands brand-name shoes, ask him or her to find something similar but less costly. If he or she does, consider putting the difference into his or her savings account.

Help motivate each of your children to put away money for certain goals within a set time frame. To make a goal tangible, have a child write it down. For someone under age ten, an objective for a baseball glove needs to be attainable in one year. For a teen's goal of a down payment for a car, set the goal further out.

At age eleven or twelve, children have the math skills to understand bigger numbers, like tens of thousands of dollars. Put their skills to work. In August, have your daughter make a list of everything she needs for school. Give her a budget, say $500. She'll quickly see that she can get three pairs of jeans at one store for the price of one pair at another.

Between the ages of eleven to thirteen, once you are confident a child can handle the responsibility, add money for clothing to an allowance. To establish a baseline, see how much money you spent on a child's clothes the previous year. Apart from big ticket basic items, such as a coat, shoes, a special event dress, or a sports jacket, let a child decide how to spend it and make his or her mistakes. Discuss what types of clothes your child is allowed to purchase.

Although making suggestions is a good idea, let your children make mistakes with their allowances. While they are young and the sums involved are modest, let them spend their allowance on things they want, and learn from their bad choices.

It will likely be difficult for you to watch a ten-year-old buy a piece of overpriced junk and be unable to go to the movies. However, experience is an effective way for children to become more discerning consumers; they will learn more from their own mistakes than from a lecture. Calmly discuss the loss, but let him or her learn the consequences of foolish monetary decisions.

One difficulty: Will you bail out your teen when he runs out of cash before his next monthly allowance and whines about how your stinginess is ruining his life? Stand firm and do not bail him out if he buys idiotic things. If you bail him out now by providing more funds to make up for irresponsible spending, he won't learn responsibility and you will likely be forced to continue to bail him out later.

To reduce the likelihood of your children continuing to be a financial drain as adults, encourage them to develop good financial habits early on. They must learn to budget, delay gratification, and make sensible money choices.

For a thirteen- to fifteen-year-old, pay a monthly allowance; again, draw up a list of expenses: clothing, entertainment, transportation, hobbies, and special events. An allowance paid monthly encourages longer-range planning and budgeting.

Most teens are responsible with money. One survey of teen spending at a mall showed that, without exception, kids were price conscious and spent less money when shopping alone or with friends than if their parents accompanied them and paid for the merchandise.

If your teens want big-ticket items (other than basics and necessities, such as a coat or shoes), which are beyond their allowance, insist that they earn the extra money by working around the house doing chores or taking a part-time or summer job. Learn to say "No," responding: "I want to give you ability to handle money responsibly, to make good choices and differentiate between your wants and your needs. I want you to contribute some part of the money to buy the things you want. Working for things is an essential adult habit." Before they start to work, come up with an understanding about how much you would like them to save and for what—college or a car.

If your fourteen-year-old wants to go on an expensive trip, tell him, "I'll pay half, but I need you to tell me how this will help you." Your child should be able to articulate why he or she should be able to go on this trip, and what he or she expects to get out of it. Ask your child, "Are you willing to give up something else to go on this trip?" Also ask, "Will you earn some extra money from a part-time or a summer job?" However, don't push part-time work too much; otherwise, your teen may find working at the mall more seductive than working toward good grades.

If you're uncomfortable about giving a larger birthday or holiday gift without any strings, exercise a measure of control by tying this type of monetary gift to something toward which your youngster is already saving. A matching gift is more likely to be spent for its intended purpose.

A teen who will inherit a large sum of money at age twenty-one needs much more than a modest allowance to prepare for the magnitude of what he or she will soon receive. In this situation, your sixteen-year-old may be able to handle an allowance of $200 per month, perhaps paid quarterly. Encourage your child to think in larger terms about saving and charitable giving, topics discussed later in this chapter. However, let your child learn from his or her own choices and mistakes.

Credit Cards

WE WERE HORRIFIED when a gleeful thirteen-year-old relative crowed that it was just so nice not to have to ask her parents for money anymore; she could just use an ATM card on their checking account. It didn't take too long before the parents rethought this tactic.

Don't give a child a credit or ATM card until high school. If your child has a checking account, begin with a debit or ATM card that runs dry once the limit is reached on funds deposited in the bank. Your teen will have an experience similar to a credit card, making him or her feel more grown up, but with a far lower liability ceiling. It's like training wheels for a credit card.

Again, try to be a role model for your children. Let them hear you discuss how you spend your money and your past spending mistakes using credit cards.

When you allow use of a credit card, don't let a child rack up endless charges on the card you provide and pay for them, otherwise his or her desires will be limitless and spending painless. Hold your teen accountable for paying any charges out of his or her allowance or earned income. Explain the importance of a good credit history. Each month go over your child's credit card statement and discuss the purchases. Ask: "Are you happy with how you spent your money? What will you do differently next month?"

In addition to going over monthly statements with them, instruct them on what to do if a card is lost or stolen. Be aware of any signs of identity theft, and check each teen's credit report annually for any unauthorized accounts.

Charitable Giving

PART OF AN allowance ought to be set aside for charitable giving and saving. Many families require between 5 and 10 percent of the allowance be set aside for charity.

Give a child an allowance in denominations that encourage charitable giving and saving, as well as immediate spending. If a youngster gets $5, give five singles. *Remember*: A kid is a kid. But don't make the process so complicated that everyone winds up frustrated.

Encourage charitable giving by ages five and six, about the same time as you start an allowance. Teach him or her to give part of his or her allowance to help alleviate the want of others who are in need.

By teaching philanthropy from an early age, the habit becomes part of the child's nature later in life. Demonstrate that a portion of one's resources is for one's own use and part is for society's; that wealth comes with responsibility. Giving part of an allowance to charity starts children thinking in the right direction. Don't wait until the teen years to impart these values; by then, a desire to instill a philanthropic bent must go against big competing forces, such as college, careers, and relationships.

For a seven-year-old, collect the cash your child has saved and wishes to donate and write a check to the chosen charity. Better yet, bring them to the charitable organization to donate the money personally. It makes a far greater impact than a parent writing a check. Let a child establish his or her own priorities, remembering that a child's interests may not coincide with yours. Give each child the freedom to be different. Even if the charity is not your choice, don't discourage your child. By finding out why the charity is of interest to him or her, you can learn a great deal about a child's thinking and emerging development. To encourage charitable giving, offer to match a child's donation to a cause of his or her choice, if he or she tells you why the cause is important.

Start younger children on a giving program that reflects their level of understanding, such as a local animal shelter. Helping children stay within their areas of interest forges a more meaningful, longer lasting connection with one charity and, more generally, to charitable giving. Beginning with one or two causes will often lead to a broader understanding of the possibilities for giving in teen years.

For children ten- to twelve-years-old, consider starting a family-giving circle to promote philanthropy. Set aside an amount that will be given away by the entire family and schedule a meeting in December to discuss what causes each family member feels strongly about. Together, work out the donations.

Use various strategies for your teens. Fund a summer trip for your teen that is both fun and offers an opportunity to give back to others. Donate to a local, child-friendly organization in your community and introduce your child to children of the same age who have developed a philanthropic bent. Encourage a teen to look at local programs that match his or her interests, have him or her call for materials from each organization or go on the Internet, and follow up with visits to programs of interest.

In summary, help your children see how you balance spending with savings and donations to charities. Try not to live as if owning the most expensive of everything is your top priority in life. Your lifestyle reflects the virtues you transmit to your children. If you live an over-the-top, extravagant lifestyle, your offspring will think it is okay and will aspire to do as you do. Conspicuous consumption represents the enemy not only of wealth accumulation but also wealth preservation.

Once you begin a dialogue with your children about what else is important in their lives besides money and "stuff," you can teach them how to manage money.

Saving, Investing, and Financial Literacy

DEVELOPING A CHILD'S financial literacy requires thoughtful, consistent, engaging efforts. The skills requisite to financial literacy create a foundation of competence and self-confidence that spill over into other areas of a child's life.

Meaningful personal finance education seldom ends up on a child's school curriculum. It's not something he or she can pick up from friends.

You must assume the responsibility for teaching money management skills to your children. You need to build concrete, age-appropriate skills, beyond budgeting, delayed gratification, and the use of credit cards. Here are some age-appropriate suggestions to impart the benefits of saving and investing.

The financial lessons learned in childhood are enormously powerful. At age five, let them collect coins in a clear container. Start the habit of saving with a traditional piggy bank, a see-through container, or a jar, where a child can see the coins. Use the accumulated coins to buy a really-wanted, moderately-priced toy and gradually, to fund a savings account.

At age seven or eight, open a savings account in your child's name at a "kid-friendly" bank, with you as custodian. Explain the rudiments of interest. When opening a savings account, shop around and locate a convenient bank that does not charge monthly fees. Encourage making regular deposits from the child's allowance or birthday checks from Grandma. Ten to 20 percent of an allowance should be saved in an interest-bearing savings account.

If your child does not want to open a savings account but wants to keep coins in his room, tell him: "We give an allowance so you can learn money management. Putting it in a bank is preferable to leaving it in a piggy bank." When you and your child are in a joyful mood, go to a bank and open the account.

At ages nine to ten, help them with a basic household budget. Introduce the concepts of risk and reward.

Ages ten to twelve are usually the best spot for teaching a range of financial skills. By the fifth grade, most children have the math skills to calculate interest and make simple budgets. At age eleven, begin to introduce stock market basics, such as what makes the price of a stock go up or down, and how to read the financial pages. Teach them about compound interest. Introduce them to something riskier than a savings account. You want them to learn to take risks, but take them prudently. That means venturing beyond the safety of a savings account. With their savings, help them buy a mutual fund with a low initial minimum investment or shares of a company he or she is interested in or a local company that he or she has heard about. Hundreds of companies sell shares directly. Companies with direct purchase plans have different minimum investment requirements and fees, among other plan details. Go over the company's annual report with your youngster.

A mutual fund is an excellent place for young investors to start because it typically invests in a portfolio of stocks in a variety of sectors. Select a no-load fund, one that does not charge an up-front commission, and open a custodial account. Let a child see how money regularly invested in a mutual fund rapidly accumulates.

At age twelve, when you start allowances twice a month, encourage making some money outside your home, by babysitting, mowing lawns, washing cars, or taking in mail for neighbors who are on vacation. With the added income, open a checking account and discuss the rules for writing checks. Introducing a checking account allows you to teach more financial basics, such as balancing a checkbook. Many banks charge monthly fees if there isn't a minimum balance; some will waive the fee if you have an account there. You may need to open a joint or custodial checking account or try a credit union.

At ages thirteen to fifteen when you begin a monthly allowance, add more to the investment basics, such as bonds, how to balance a portfolio, and how to research stocks and mutual funds. Introduce a debit card if your teen has a checking account; otherwise, start with a pre-paid card, which also limits a child's spending. A debit or prepaid card gives your youngster access to emergency funds without the need to carry cash. By opening a checking account with a debit-card privilege, you're helping educate your child about banking. Each month, review the child's spending history with him or her.

When your child is a teen, talk about your own finances, your successes, and—equally important—your failures.

At ages sixteen to eighteen, if your child has a part-time or summer job, beyond saving a part for college, encourage him or her to invest part of his or her earnings in a Roth IRA. Although a teen may think it ludicrous to contemplate retirement savings, illustrate the huge pay-off from the power of compounding over half a century. Time is definitely on their side. Have your child put some of his or her earnings into a Roth IRA and fund the rest, up to what your child earned or the current annual maximum, whichever is less. Keep records of the amounts earned. Also, discuss the tax-related issues appearing on a paycheck.

Consider giving a sixteen- or seventeen-year-old a voice in significant family financial decisions. Why? It tells him or her that this is something he or she should be aware of and that in the future he or she will need to make these types of decisions.

In short, before college, your teen needs to know how to save, spend wisely, earn, and talk about money.

During the college years, introduce them to your family's financial plans and their place in these plans. Let them work with your family's financial advisor to develop a greater level of sophistication in money management and to begin to learn how financial advisors work.

Offer the same financial lessons to your sons and daughters. Both need training in saving and investing for the future. Financial literacy and some knowledge about money management are essential to gender equality—don't let your daughter feel inferior to your son about her financial skills; she needs to feel comfortable handling money. Don't let your daughter grow up assuming her husband will manage the family finances. Give both your sons and daughters equal encouragement to save. Use eBay as a marketplace to teach lessons about wheeling and dealing.

Some of your children may be oblivious and stubbornly refuse to focus on money. Encourage each child, even if only interested in sports or music, to gain some knowledge of the financial world.

Be a role model. Let your children see how both parents take an active role in the family's finances and in making key investment decisions, even if Mom pays the bills and Dad implements the decisions. Let them see that financial responsibilities ought to be shared and that financial roles are often blurred.

Entrepreneurship

ENTREPRENEURIAL URGES MAY show up between ages ten and twelve. To promote the entrepreneurial spirit, encourage your ten- to twelve-year-old to turn a talent, interest, or passion into a small business venture. Be prepared to buy a lot of lemonade, Girl Scout cookies and other edibles.

Encourage, as age-appropriate, money-making projects. These projects provide an opportunity for you to talk about various aspects of a business, including how to market the venture and set a price that will turn a profit. Let them see that making money does not come easily and that they must work for what they want.

If your eleven-year-old wants to set up a fresh-squeezed orange juice stand, encourage her. It is a teachable mo-

ment. Work with her on a business plan, including pur-
chasing the ingredients and determining how much to
charge. Help her locate a place for the stand where there
is likely to be a lot of foot traffic.

EBay offers wonderful opportunities to hone a child's
entrepreneurial skills, for example, by selling unwanted
games. But remember, you must stay in charge.

Sources for Financial Learning and Entrepreneurship

THE PROLIFERATION OF personal finance materials makes
it easier for you to teach financial concepts at home. Resources include interactive Internet games, stock market
simulations, and workbooks. Avoid idiotic investment
games that often encourage high short-term returns by
taking absurd risks. Start by looking at Jump$tart Coali-
tion for Financial Literacy's Web site (*www.jumpstartcoali-
tion.org*), which lists information on hundreds of publica-
tions and other materials, evaluated by an educational
consultant for objectivity, with the ability to spark a child's
interest and independence from specific financial products. The search can be narrowed by age and by topic.
Beware of Web sites and materials developed by financial
institutions that seek to promote financial literacy as good
public relations and a way to attract customers. Because
these firms have products they want to sell, their financial
literacy services are usually self-promotional.

As parents seek out the best coaches and finest musical instruments for their children, wanting their children
to be better prepared, they increasingly give financial development a similar level of attention and support. You

can send your children to special summer camps to learn money management and entrepreneurial skills. Some personal finance or entrepreneurship camps look to develop personal financial literacy or educate on global financial markets; others focus on how to start a small business venture.

For high-net-worth families (say, those with $10 million or more), financial institutions offer wealth education programs for children and young adults. The players include specialized firms as well as banks and trust companies. Although serving as marketing tools for the next generation of clients, the best programs offer several classes over a longer period of at least one year, and hands-on experience in learning about investments, starting a business, or running a family company.

Don't overlook Grandma and Grandpa in your children's financial education. Make sure they are part of your training process. Grandparents may offer an advantage over parents when giving financial advice to young adults. When parents talk about finances with their kids, sometimes there is a lot of emotion involved. A grandparent offers emotional distance and may find a more receptive audience.

7 Wealth Transfer Basics: How to Better Understand Your Attorney, Accountant, and Financial Planner

A sixty-two-year-old woman friend of ours suddenly lost her husband after 41 years of marriage. She had gone directly from her family's gracious home to live with her husband, who handled all financial matters.

When we offered our condolences and asked if there was any way we could help her, she promptly replied: "Help me understand my finances! I don't even know what questions to ask or whom to ask. I just want to know if I have enough money to pay my bills. I don't even know if I need an attorney or an accountant and I have no idea what a financial planner does. What do I do first?" This grieving widow was about to enter the world of personal finance and estate planning, which can be daunting and rather complex for everyone, but especially for people with significant assets.

This chapter is designed to introduce you to some wealth transfer basics so you can ask the right questions and better understand your options when you talk with your attorney, accountant, and financial planner. Many people assume that if there is a crisis, their children will take care of it. They say, "I trust in God and my family." But it's a huge mistake. The more money you have, the sooner you need to think about estate and financial planning documents. Considered in this chapter are: a will, a power of attorney, a trust, a living will, a health care proxy, and a 529 plan. Also discussed is the advisability of making outright gifts to adult children and grandchildren, a topic considered in more detail in Chapter 8.

Keep in mind the story of Charlie, who unexpectedly died in his early forties before doing any planning. Because he did not have a will, under local law, Charlie's multimillion dollar estate was divided equally between his widow and two toddlers, triggering a huge estate tax and leaving his widow without enough money to pay expenses. As minors, the children had to have court-appointed guardians to oversee their inheritance until they each turned eighteen. At that point, the children controlled their money, but were not prepared to handle it (see Chapter 8).

What Is a Will?

A WILL IS a legal document prepared while you are alive that directs what happens to your assets after your death. It allows you to designate an executor (now called a personal representative in many states) who will administer your estate.

It also allows you to designate a guardian for your minor children. There is no perfect person who can care for your minor children the way you do. Pick a guardian who is young enough to outlive the responsibilities and shares your emphasis on positive character traits, among other things.

Your will cannot control what is done with your body or how your funeral is arranged. Also, give a letter covering these matters to your relatives and your executor. Also, give your executor a letter listing: your key advisors, the location of important documents, a list of your assets (and any advice on how to handle certain assets, such as collectibles) and liabilities, the location of your safe deposit box, the code to an in-home safe, and online account passwords.

What Is a Power of Attorney?

A POWER OF attorney gives the power holder the authority to manage your finances if you are disabled. Otherwise, if you haven't made plans or assets aren't in joint names, your loved ones must go to court to have someone designated to handle your finances, which is a time-consuming and often emotionally draining and costly process.

Beware of whom you designate as your agent (more technically, your attorney-in-fact), especially in a blended family situation. Soon after ailing Mary gave her second husband her power of attorney, he transferred the family home, which she owned, into his name. After Mary's death six months later, the transfer enraged Mary's only child, Scott, who insisted she meant to leave the house to him. Think carefully about giving certain "hot" powers, such as making gifts, changing beneficiaries on life insurance, or retitling brokerage accounts, which are dangerous in the hands of an abuser who thinks it's his or her money.

There are two types of powers. Most states recognize a durable power of attorney, which takes effect immediately and stays in effect unless you revoke it. Some states only recognize a springing power that takes effect when you are disabled. A springing power requires your agent to get a physician to certify that you are not mentally competent.

You also need to pick an agent you can trust. He or she ought to be detail-oriented. Operating without official oversight requires honesty. You may want to name a primary agent and a backup agent. You probably will want your primary agent to act individually in most situations, but the two must act jointly to make a gift or sell property. Thus, big decisions, such as signing a deed to sell your home and give away the proceeds, would have to be made jointly.

A power of attorney can be general or specific. Consult your attorney who will probably recommend a general power because you cannot anticipate all the issues that might arise.

Beware: Most financial institutions require you to use their own power of attorney form. They likely will reject a power of attorney drafted by your lawyer.

What Is a Trust?

A TRUST IS an arrangement that involves a transfer by you (the settlor or grantor) of some of your assets to a trustee who will hold them for a beneficiary (you, others, your survivors, or some combination of these), according to your instructions. The trustee manages the trust property according to the trust agreement and state law and also handles administrative work, such as filing any necessary tax returns.

There are two types of trusts: testamentary and living. A trust you create in your will is a testamentary trust. This type of trust comes into action after your death.

A living trust is one you create while you are alive. You can serve as your own trustee (or as a cotrustee) or name another person or a financial institution to serve as the trustee. Once you create a living trust, you typically fund it with securities and cash. However, you can fund it with nearly any asset provided the trustee is willing to receive it.

A living trust holds assets during your lifetime and distributes them after your death. Assets placed in a living trust will pass to future generations according to terms of the trust agreement, not your will. Any assets held in a living trust at the time of your death avoid the probate process. Probate refers to the judicial process for: determining the validity of your will, collecting and disposing of your assets passing under your will, paying claims, and distributing your estate as directed by your will. The probate process is costly and time-consuming, unless your state has streamlined the procedures and made the costs reasonable.

A living trust is a useful means of controlling and managing your assets if you become disabled. Remember to name someone else as a successor trustee (or a cotrustee with you) and have the successor (or cotrustee) take over under the terms of the trust agreement if you become disabled (or no longer wish to act as trustee), thereby freeing you from investment responsibilities and details.

Recall from earlier in this chapter what Charlie should have done. A living trust is a wonderful alternative to guardianship for the property of your minor children. Rather than designating a guardian of the property for your minor children in your will, it is better to set up trust for their care. Consult your attorney. To create a system of checks and balances, the guardian of the person and the trustee probably should not be the same person.

Remember to retitle assets you wish to place in a living trust. It's easy with a brokerage account; fill out an application in the trust's name. For real estate, have your attorney prepare a new deed.

A living trust may be irrevocable or revocable. An irrevocable trust requires you to completely surrender control over property you transfer to the trust. Because this type of trust cannot be changed once created, only set up an irrevocable trust if you are certain you will not need the trust property in the future. If you are subject to federal estate taxes, your tax advisor may suggest an irrevocable trust for your life insurance policies to exclude the proceeds from your estate and thus save taxes. Talk to your advisor about the details.

A revocable living trust allows you (the settlor creating the trust) to change the trust terms, such as to whom, how, and when assets will pass during your lifetime or on your death. You can remove trust property placed in a revocable trust. You can also terminate a revocable trust and take back the trust property.

Because a revocable, living trust avoids the probate process, it achieves privacy, if that is a desired objective. Unlike a will, a living trust is not filed publicly. Thus, the public cannot ascertain how trust assets are distributed to the beneficiaries of a revocable, living trust.

If You Have a Living Trust, Do You Need a Will?

AFTER YOU CREATE a living trust, assets, such as your personal effects, may be held outside the trust. You will need a will to distribute property that you do not place in trust during your lifetime or you may want to transfer ownership of certain noninvestment assets, such as your car, to the trust.

Do Your Living Trust and Your Will Control Your Entire Estate?

NO. JOINTLY HELD property generally goes to the survivor. Life insurance and retirement plan benefits are payable to the named beneficiaries. For assets not covered by your will and living trust, review your beneficiary designations periodically. In addition to your primary beneficiary, name contingent beneficiaries.

What Is a Living Will?

A LIVING WILL is a document, an advance directive, which states your wishes about how you want to be cared for at the end of your life. It lists your general preferences for or against various life-prolonging treatments. Basically, in preparing your living will you must consider if you want to stop or remove medical care (if so, in what circumstances) or if you want care in nearly all circumstances. Because a simple living will may be difficult to apply in many circumstances, you may need a customized living will. Talk to your attorney, but remember a living will is often ineffective. Sometimes a physician will see it *after* administering a treatment, or simply ignore it.

What Is a Health Care Proxy?

A HEALTH CARE proxy (sometimes called a health care power of attorney) designates someone whom you trust (your proxy) to voice your wishes and make medical care decisions when you are unable to do so. If you have a choice of agents, go for someone smart, who is not afraid of authority and can deal with a hospital's bureaucracy. All of your physicians and your proxy (or proxies) should have a copy of your health care proxy.

Should You Make Gifts to Your Adult Children?

THE PRACTICE OF giving while one is alive is gaining momentum. Think about giving "with a warm heart, not a cold hand." Many people enjoy seeing their children and grandchildren benefiting from their largesse and like receiving recognition for their gifts.

Today, your children may be in their sixties before they receive their inheritance on your demise. Consider whether outright gifts will make life easier for them earlier. For example, gifts can help your children make a down payment on a first home, reduce (or eliminate) the debt burden of graduate school, or seed (or enhance) a first business venture. Discuss with your children any conditions on your gifts. For instance, does a gift for a down payment on a home come with the expectation that it will be used to buy a home in a certain location or price range? Be specific as to your conditions or expectations.

Gift giving will enable you to see how your adult children (and adult grandchildren) handle assets. Start with small, but meaningful, gifts. If you think someone handles a gift inappropriately, consider making future wealth transfer through a trust, as discussed in Chapter 8.

However, your well-intentioned gifts may be too much of a good thing that can hurt your children in the long run. Regular gifts may encourage a lifestyle your son cannot afford or send a message to your daughter that she cannot care for herself. Use gifts to help your children become independent, not to maintain their dependency. We assume that you want your adult children to be economically self-sufficient and that you do not believe you owe your children a "lifestyle."

Regardless of your adult children's maturity and financial responsibility, only give away cash or other assets that you can afford to live without. Don't give away so much that your standard of living is at risk. Retain sufficient assets to finance the long lifespan you and your spouse will likely enjoy.

If you go the outright gift giving route, you should be aware of some federal wealth transfer tax basics. A gift of cash or property can help you avoid federal gift and estate taxes. The longer you hold appreciating assets, the higher the eventual federal wealth transfer taxes will likely be. It can make sense to give away some assets that are not needed to maintain your current lifestyle.

You can give each of your children (and grandchildren) free of federal gift taxes up to a specified amount of cash or certain property interests annually. This is known as the gift tax annual per donee exclusion. The annual exclusion amount increases in thousand dollar increments due to inflation adjustments. For a married couple, the annual per donee exclusion is doubled if your spouse consents to "split" a gift to any individual. Your tax advisor can fill you in on the details and any IRS forms you need to file.

You and your spouse each have a lifetime credit against the federal gift tax, thereby providing for a lifetime exclusion from federal gift taxation of a specified dollar amount of taxable gifts (in excess of the annual per donee exclusion). Thus, if you make a taxable gift above the annual exclusion amount, the credit used to offset your federal gift tax liability in one year reduces the amount of credit that can be used against the gift tax in a subsequent year. Only after you exhaust your lifetime exemption are gifts above the annual exclusion amount subject to federal gift taxation. Again, consult your tax advisor.

What Is a 529 Plan?

WITH ONE YEAR of undergraduate tuition, room, and board (not to mention books, lab fees, and other miscellaneous expenses) at a private university costing about $50,000 and going ever higher, it's never too early to start saving. So get a Social Security number for every one of your newborns as soon as they come home from the hospital and start contributing before they are out of diapers. But how?

Section 529 plans, which come from Section 529 of the Internal Revenue Code, provide some favorable and unique tax advantages not offered by the other college-savings options. These plans allow anyone, regardless of their income or their age, to save tax-free for skyrocketing higher education expenses, by investing in a plan's menu of mutual funds.

There are two types of 529 plans: prepaid tuition plans and savings plans. States can sponsor prepayment and savings plans; private colleges can set up prepayment plans. A prepaid tuition plan allows you to pay a child's (or grandchild's) undergraduate tuition in advance at a designated higher education institution. By locking in the current tuition rate, you avoid spiraling tuition costs.

You probably want the more popular option: a savings plan that allows parents and grandparents to invest in a tax-free investment account, where the savings grow free from federal income taxes (and generally from state and local income taxes) without being locked into a specific higher education institution.

Although plans typically have high contribution limits, $250,000 or $300,000, you can accumulate substantial sums in these tax sheltered accounts for a beneficiary's college and graduate school expenses. When used to pay for the plan beneficiary's qualifying higher education expenses, including tuition and other costs, such as room and board, funds distributed from a 529 plan are free from federal income taxes (and generally from state and local income taxes).

Although 529 plans are state-sponsored, you can invest in any plan wherever you live. Money invested in a 529 plan can be used for public or private postsecondary institutions in any state.

Many states offer an immediate income tax deduction, up to a maximum amount, for residents who make contributions to their state-sponsored 529 plan. Unless your state's plan charges high fees or otherwise imposes burdensome restrictions, consider funding an in-state plan up to the deduction amount. Then look at both in- and out-of-state plans, focusing on: fees, investment options, contributions limits, and penalties for moving an account. Although some plans are available only through brokers, try to skirt the sales fee typically levied when a plan is sold by a financial advisor by dealing directly with a state or a mutual fund organization. A few states even offer the option of taking an income tax deduction for contributions to any state's plan.

Because contributions can be treated as if made over a five-year period, a 529 plan offers federal gift tax advantages. You can superfund a 529 plan by contributing five times the annual per donee exclusion amount in one year without triggering federal gift taxes. Consult your tax advisor for details as well as how you and your spouse can contribute ten times the annual per donee exclusion amount gift tax-free in any one year. Also, the account balance in a 529 plan is generally not included in your estate for federal estate tax purposes. However, if you superfund a 529 plan and die within five years of making the contribution, part of the gift is included in your estate for federal estate tax purposes. Again, consult your tax advisor.

You, as the plan owner, can change the plan beneficiary. If the initial beneficiary does not go to college, you can name another beneficiary.

Most states require the balance in a plan account be spent within a specified time frame, say the thirtieth birthday of the beneficiary. Other states place a time limit on each plan, for example, ten years after the beneficiary's high school graduation or college enrollment.

Sometimes a state changes its plan or another jurisdiction makes its plan more attractive. Subject to certain restrictions, you can make a tax-free rollover from one state's plan to another (or from one plan to another one within the same state).

What's the catch? Only cash can be invested in a 529 plan. Each state determines the investment choices, providing a limited number of options, including investments based on the beneficiary's age. Under the latter option, the asset manager will shift holdings to less-aggressive investments as the beneficiary grows up so by the time the money is needed the account hopefully will be less vulnerable to stock market volatility.

Watch for state-imposed restrictions on withdrawals and rollovers. Avoid opening an account in a plan with a sales charge, high enrollment and maintenance fees, or high investment management expenses. High fees can erode, and in some cases even erase, a plan's tax-saving benefits. If you have had good experiences with certain big mutual fund companies, look to them as plan investment managers.

Some states that allow state income tax deductions for contributions to Section 529 plans provide for the recapture of these deductions if you prematurely liquidate an account or transfer the account to another state's plan.

What Is the Unlimited Education Exclusion?

REGARDLESS OF THE amount of a private school or a college's tuition and fees, payments you make directly to an educational institution are exempt from federal gift taxation. This is an attractive option for parents and grandparents, enabling them to fund educational expenses and to make their estates smaller, if they are subject to federal estate taxation. *Remember:* You must write the check directly to the private school, college, or graduate school.

8 How to Use Trusts to Transfer Your Wealth to Your Children and Grandchildren

Ken loved to bet on sports, horses, and almost anything else. He had a shaky work history and limited retirement savings. His aging parents feared that an outright cash inheritance would be squandered in a few trips to Las Vegas. So Ken's parents set up a trust for him.

So, too, you should consider a trust rather than making outright gifts to your children and grandchildren. Rather than giving assets now or leaving property outright on your death, trusts provide more options. Trusts have controls, limits, and time lines.

Simply because a child or grandchild reaches the age of majority does not mean that the young adult is ready or able to manage substantial assets. Leaving aside federal wealth tax considerations, large, outright transfers, during your life or on your death, may also sap motivation or encourage reckless spending. In short, money may present a challenge to one's character.

When fifty-year-old Pat inherited a modest cash amount on his mother's death, he immediately spent it all on a luxury car with all the bells and whistles, rather than saving it for his retirement years.

Do your children or grandchildren have a "windfall mentality?" Those who do will not properly manage a large windfall for the long term. They will increase their spending or buy items they would not purchase with their own income or assets. Those with a windfall mentality usually go through gifts or an inheritance fairly quickly.

If you do not want the wealth you transfer to your children or grandchildren to be treated as a windfall and feel your loved ones will not manage it properly, consider a trust. A trust can be structured to limit spending and preserve assets.

Apart from spending to indulge their proclivities, your loved ones may lack the knowledge or maturity to manage money. They may need investment professionals to manage the money you transfer to them. They may need a trust that controls the money until they are mature enough to invest responsibly.

If wealth is received and retained in trust, your views regarding the preservation of wealth and the passing of assets to succeeding generations are more likely to be observed. A trust may also provide professional management and administration. However, fees for a trust can pile up, especially if the trustee is a financial institution.

Assets placed in a living trust are protected not only from mistakes resulting from a child's immaturity or poor judgment but also from probate. As noted in Chapter 7, avoidance of probate preserves privacy, reduces expenses, and generally results in the more expedient administration of assets. On the death of a beneficiary, a living trust can continue to administer assets, if you wish, privately and without court involvement for the successor beneficiaries.

Different types of trusts provide protections and structure for children and grandchildren that outright transfers, which provide unfettered access to funds, cannot. This chapter considers six types of trusts: discretionary, incentive, total return, stepping stone, dynasty, and special needs. Some suggestions for selecting trustees are also presented as well as the need for a letter of instructions.

Remember: Not all your children (or grandchildren) are the same, nor are they likely to find themselves in similar circumstances. In formulating a wealth transfer plan, you need to take into account the needs, interests, and strengths of the various individuals involved.

Discretionary Trusts

KEN, THE GAMBLER described at the beginning of this chapter, was the beneficiary of a discretionary trust his parents created for him, meaning he had to ask the trustee each time he wanted money. His parents stipulated in the trust document that the money paid out to Ken had to be for a specific and legitimate purpose.

With a discretionary trust, the trustee has the power— the discretion—to pay (or not pay) income and/or principal to the beneficiary or among the beneficiaries and accumulate any undistributed income.

For this type of trust to work, you must provide guidelines about your concerns and objectives for your trustee to follow. You may want your trustee to make distributions, for example, to ensure educational opportunities, health care, and reasonable housing. You may desire your trustee to provide funds for a wealth-creating venture, if a young adult develops a business plan and has had experience in the desired field. To encourage gainful employment, you could direct your trustee to make generous distributions up to (and even above) a child's salary, but be strict in making distributions to a child who is not gainfully employed, provided he or she is not disabled. You may want to direct your trustee to refrain from most distributions to a beneficiary at a specified age who has not found employment.

Because it's impossible to anticipate all future possibilities, the choice of a trustee is important. Disputes about trust language sometimes cause the trustee and the beneficiary to become adversaries.

In a total discretionary trust, the determination of the amount and the timing of the distributions are left to the trustee. This permits maximum flexibility in dealing with future circumstances. It also provides the ultimate in creditor and divorce claims protection, because the beneficiary lacks any enforceable rights against the trust. With this type of discretionary trust, if Ken's wife grew tired of his gambling and divorced him, she could not access his trust. If asset protection is a concern, consult your attorney.

Naming multiple beneficiaries, for example, a child who receives the income and a grandchild who will receive the principal, may create problems. Make your preferences clear in the guidelines you give to your trustee as to how you want to balance the needs of the current income beneficiary and those of the future beneficiary of the trust principal.

Incentive Trusts

NICK WAS A member of a very wealthy family. He was quite intelligent and had earned an MBA from an Ivy League school. Physically healthy and the beneficiary of a trust, he spent his time flying airplanes, riding horses, and driving sports cars. Yet he never seemed happy.

An incentive trust has become popular as a way for wealth holders to transfer virtues and goals to children and grandchildren. People want to be generous, but they want assurances that their wealth will not be wasted. They are concerned that inheriting wealth will reduce a child or grandchild's work ethic. They are fearful money will disappear in a spending spree or go to an ex-spouse.

Robbed of the incentive to earn a living, trust fund babies such as Nick, often lead consumption-oriented lives, working at nothing, taking no risks, overcoming no challenges, creating and producing little. They wind up unfulfilled and suffer from poor self-esteem.

An incentive trust is expressly designed to influence a beneficiary's behavior. This type of trust sets specific, hopefully measurable, criteria for a beneficiary's conduct. An incentive trust will enable you to convey your virtues, for example, the desirability of gainful employment, to your beneficiaries. You will give them the money provided they play by your rules.

An incentive trust is basically a discretionary trust defined to specify behavior you want to influence, promote, or discourage in your beneficiary. You need to articulate your goals and priorities, such as gainful employment, business achievement, academic excellence, social contribution or dedication to family. You create certain goals a beneficiary must achieve to qualify for trust distributions—income and/or principal—thereby protecting the value of trust assets and fostering character traits that are meaningful to you.

If you are concerned about young children and grandchildren who grow up in a privileged environment, you need to think about the distribution guidelines that serve as a roadmap for administering the trust. For example, you may want to fund a beneficiary's education. However, do you have more specific educational objectives in mind?

In replacing trustee discretion with measurable targets, a need exists for objective criteria: pay stubs, transcripts, drug tests. Clearly understood and determinable standards for distributions make it harder for a beneficiary to use ambiguity in a trust instrument to extract discretionary distributions. The aim is to encourage the beneficiary to meet objective standards of good behavior (or refrain from bad behavior) as established by you, the settlor.

However, an incentive trust can be a minefield. Although providing guidance to your trustee regarding your goals, this type of trust should not be too rigid. Incentive trusts often suffer from a lack of flexibility; problems of measurement and enforcement may also arise.

Granting a monetary reward for certain achievements, such as graduation from college, may create unnecessary stress for beneficiaries. You may want to grant a monetary reward for graduating college or a trade school (such as a cooking or art school), or even reaching a certain age (see Stepping Stone Trusts, discussed later in this chapter). What if a beneficiary becomes disabled? An education-oriented trust can backfire, for instance, if a beneficiary develops a learning disability that keeps him or her from graduating from college.

In considering an incentive trust, ask yourself: do you want to control a beneficiary's life by specifying the conditions that he or she must meet before receiving distributions? For example, do you want to tie distributions to a beneficiary graduating from college with a specified grade point average or a beneficiary's earning power, with the payout matching his or her annual job income?

Beware: If not properly designed, an incentive trust can unfairly reward certain beneficiaries or punish others in a way that you never intended, fueling inequities and family resentments. Take the "earn a dollar, get a dollar" type trust. If one child becomes an investment banker and another a school teacher, the banker may receive large distributions he or she may not need, while the teacher will get far less from the trust, despite having a greater need. Furthermore, unless other provisions are made, homemakers and volunteers may get nothing from this type of trust.

Caution must be exercised with respect to punitive provisions designed to discourage negative behavior, such as substance abuse. This type of provision may drive a wedge between the beneficiary and the trustee, leading the beneficiary to be more secretive about his or her behavior and not pursue counseling or treatment. Wishing a beneficiary to be drug free will likely require regular testing. This provision will likely be seen as degrading, thereby fueling a beneficiary's bitterness.

The choice of a trustee is critical for an incentive trust. Naming one child as trustee for the benefit of his or her siblings can be a recipe for disaster. Looking to a corporate or nonfamily member trustee often presents a challenge for the trustee in difficult situations. Select someone who is up to the job, someone who is firm, but fair. To avoid any misunderstandings and lessen the potential for litigation, build a conflict resolution system into the trust so that the resolution of any disputes becomes standardized and not arbitrary.

You probably believe, as we do, that people respond to incentives. An incentive trust provides a vehicle to communicate your virtues and goals to your children and grandchildren. But your offspring may be resentful if they feel that you did not trust them. As trust beneficiaries, your children and grandchildren may resent you for trying to control them from the grave with money.

Before you go the incentive trust route, consider a few issues. Does it imply distrust? Is the trust you wish to establish too inflexible, complex, or difficult to administer? Never use an incentive trust to try to control a child's choice of spouse or religious faith.

Total Return Trusts

A YOUNG WIDOW with three children, Peggy chose a career in social work, a field she loved but which didn't provide her with sufficient income for her family. Her affluent parents applauded her career and hard work, but set up a trust designed to meet the financial needs of Peggy and her children by providing for monthly income payments.

Traditionally, you could structure a trust to distribute some or all of the trust income to current beneficiaries, such as Peggy. This worked well with relatively high dividend yields on common stock, say of 5 percent. Today, with lower dividend yields, the income beneficiaries will receive far lower payments from the trust. Or, the trustee will invest the principal in bonds to obtain higher returns, depriving the future beneficiaries of any appreciation potential.

Planners increasingly have turned to total return trusts or unitrusts. The income beneficiary is paid a percentage of the trust's value, say 5 percent, each year. This approach allows the trustee to invest for long-term returns, rather than merely looking to invest in bonds to boost the income payments to the current beneficiary. It also allows the annual income distributions to increase as the value of the trust property appreciates and it provides a steadier income stream for a beneficiary, such as Peggy.

Also, consult your attorney for state laws that permit traditional trusts to be changed into total return trusts.

A total return trust can be coupled with giving the trustee the power to invade principal based on an ascertainable standard, such as health or education. This approach gives the beneficiary an indication that more or less regular distributions will be received, and that additional financial support may be available. However, it may be more difficult for a trustee of this type of trust to deal with changed or unforeseen circumstances than would be the case with a discretionary-type trust.

Stepping Stone Trusts

ROSALYN AND STEVE died together in an automobile crash, leaving their twenty-year-old son, Jeff, with far more money than he could handle. But luckily, Jeff's parents had wisely established a stepping stone trust that provided him with enough money to finish his education, and then provided another sum at age twenty-five so he could either start a business or continue on to graduate school. Unfortunately Jeff squandered that money, but his parents provided no additional distributions until age thirty-five. By then Jeff had matured quite a bit and learned to manage the distribution he received at thirty-five as well as the final principal distribution that he received at forty-five.

With this type of trust, the beneficiary receives the principal in stages. Because many adults have a hard time handling wealth at age twenty-one, consider, for example, handing over one-half of the principal at age thirty, with no strings attached, and the rest at age thirty-five. There's no perfect age or ages; however, you want to give a beneficiary time to mature. This type of trust hopefully allows the beneficiary to learn how to manage money. It also encourages the beneficiary to be productive and provides an incentive to succeed.

Remember: If outright distributions from a trust are made during earlier, career building years and are significantly greater than a child could realistically earn, motivation for achievement may be compromised. It is generally advisable to wait until each child reaches his or her midthirties before transferring assets outright or free of a trust. By this age, your children will likely have attained emotional maturity.

Use an Escape Clause with Stepping Stone Trusts

REGARDLESS OF HOW carefully an attorney drafts a trust, a beneficiary may be unready to handle a substantial sum of money. Many unanticipated problems can arise, such as substance abuse or gambling debts. Consider a general escape clause that allows your trustee to withhold income and/or principal payments when it is in the best interests of the beneficiary to do so. A well-drafted clause should provide that the payments will resume when the trustee determines it is in the beneficiary's best interests. Give your trustee written guidelines explaining when you think an escape clause should be used. Again, carefully select your trustee.

Conversely, you may want to authorize additional distributions in crisis situations, such as divorce, during periods of involuntary unemployment, or for counseling in the event of personal problems, such as substance abuse.

Dynasty Trusts

JOE AND CATHY, a fabulously wealthy, elderly couple, had four children, twelve grandchildren, and seven great-grandchildren. With a still growing family, a dynasty trust seemed appropriate for them.

You may want to consider a dynasty trust. This is a long-term trust that will last for several generations, even perpetually. Typically, a dynasty trust only pays out income to the current beneficiaries and retains the trust principal to generate future income. This type of trust benefits more than one generation. It allows for significant long-term growth of principal and protects against overspending or mismanagement, particularly by the first generation of beneficiaries (in this case, Joe and Cathy's children).

In the past, state laws limited how long a trust could last. However, these laws (the so-called rule against perpetuities) are passing from the scene. Some states now allow trusts to last forever; others allow trusts for 360 to 1,000 years. Consult your attorney.

Through the federal generation-skipping transfer tax, Congress sought to deal with dynasty trusts. In brief, a tax is imposed on a transfer from a grandparent to a grandchild, subject to an amount exempted from the imposition of the generation-skipping transfer tax, which could be imposed decades after the initial creation and funding of the trust. Consult an experienced tax advisor if you are planning to create a trust for your grandchildren (or succeeding generations). Typically, an irrevocable, dynasty trust will be structured to avoid federal wealth transfer taxes on your death and the demise of future generations as well as state inheritance taxes.

Long-term trusts are a problem. Your family and the law may change, among other possibilities. Don't create a trust that can't be changed in the face of unanticipated circumstances.

If you want to set up a dynasty trust to last for several generations, consider designating a protector, someone other than the trustee. You can give a protector broad or limited powers to: add or remove beneficiaries, change the age at which distributions are made or the amount of distributions, or change the trustee. Generally, select a family member, friend, or one of your professional advisors as the protector. Provide a process for selecting a successor protector.

Over the course of the existence of a dynasty trust, changes will occur in tax laws, investment practices, the family's makeup, including changes in the beneficiaries' needs and circumstances. Consult your attorney on the ways both the trustee and the beneficiary (or beneficiaries) can modify the trust to accomplish any needed changes. However, future flexibility must be balanced against the objective of carrying out your interests with regard to your wealth transfer plan.

You likely will need $5 million or more to fund a dynasty trust, which can be funded with a variety of assets. In addition to legal fees to set up the arrangement, the trust will pay annual investment management and administrative fees to the trustee, if you select a financial institution or a nonfamily member as the trustee (or co-trustee).

Locking up money for generations without knowing who will receive funds doesn't make much sense, even if you have considerable assets and are able to avoid federal wealth transfer taxes. In any event, you and your attorney must plan for the eventuality that you will have no heirs and your dynasty comes to an end.

Special Needs Trusts

CLAIRE AND ROBERT had a daughter, Jenny, who developed schizophrenia at age seventeen. For many years she lived in a protected shelter and was unable to work at anything more than very menial jobs. Even those, she couldn't hold for very long. Claire and Robert set up a special needs trust for Jenny.

A special needs trust will enable you to provide for a disabled beneficiary that governmental benefits will not cover, such as dental care, vacations, pocket money after the death of you and your spouse. Assets held in a properly drafted special needs trust do not count against the income and net worth qualifications for state-administered Medicaid programs and federal Supplemental Social Insurance payments (the latter when a disabled person turns eighteen).

Even parents of a young, disabled child should consider a special needs trust in case of a catastrophic event.

Consult a knowledgeable attorney so that the trust will sustain a child's quality of life but not jeopardize governmental benefits. Carefully select a trustee. Avoid giving or leaving money to a relative or friend with a moral obligation to take care of a disabled person.

Selection of Trustees

SELECTING THE RIGHT trustee is critical to all these trust arrangements, so don't make the selection of trustees an afterthought in your wealth transfer plan or choose a bank recommended by your attorney as trustee. Consider other options. Take your time and shop around.

You may want to establish cotrustees who have different backgrounds and perspectives. You may want someone who knows your family and is familiar with your plan—for example, a family member who can bring expertise with respect to your personal situation, your goals, and the idiosyncrasies of your loved ones. An individual who knows the day-to-day needs of your beneficiaries, will provide personalized, compassionate judgments about distributions to a beneficiary, which are hopefully consistent with your wishes. Interpersonal skills are key; so, too, is the backbone to say "No." A corporate cotrustee, such as a bank, can handle trust investments and administration.

Look to a financial institution if you anticipate that your trust will last for years, need professional investment management, or require complex record keeping and tax reporting. Check fees, investment records, and customer service. Service, now and in the future, is a concern when considering a corporate trustee. Often there are high fees and a lack of personal attention.

There are few things nastier than warring trustees who can be divided and conquered by a beneficiary to get around a trust's ambiguous guidelines. If you want more than one trustee, the trust instrument must provide how the trustees will interact and make decisions. Consider giving an individual the sole authority over distributions and a veto power over investment decisions, among other key actions. Or, you may want to name one individual as the trustee and give him or her the authority to hire a professional investment manager and a trust company to handle records and tax returns. Having two professionals, however, increases complexity and expenses and may delay the taking of trustee actions. You may want to name a protector to watch a trustee's (or the trustees') work.

An individual trustee can best serve a trust with less than $1 million that cannot justify the fees required by a corporate trustee. An individual trustee also makes sense if you expect the trust to last only a few years.

Consider the complexity and type of assets you will place in the trust. Managing a portfolio of securities differs from managing a far-flung real estate business.

You need to tailor a workable, creative trustee succession plan, for example, if an individual trustee declines to serve, resigns, becomes incompetent, dies, or is removed. Succession planning is also imperative for long-term trusts, such as a dynasty trust.

Remember: Designate how a successor trustee will be selected, especially if you designate one or more individuals as trustees. You also will need a mechanism to replace a corporate trustee if you use a financial institution.

For any trust designed to benefit multiple generations, ask your attorney about techniques to build flexibility into a trust so a beneficiary can remove a trustee and appoint a successor trustee, but not change distributions for his or her own benefit.

Prepare a Letter of Instructions

IF YOUR TRUSTEE has discretion in managing the trust and making distributions of income and/or principal, write a letter of instructions outlining your intentions and what actions you would prefer the trustee to take in various circumstances. In short, a letter of instructions articulates your wishes for your trust.

In a letter of instructions you explicitly state how you would like your trust to be managed and how you want your beneficiaries to benefit from the trust. For example, with a discretionary trust, you can use a letter of instructions to explain under what circumstances a trustee can exercise discretion to invade the trust principal for a beneficiary. This can also help the trustee formulate an investment strategy and communicate it to the beneficiary. It may also provide a beneficiary with greater insight into your intentions. These statements afford you the opportunity to make your objectives clear, even after your death.

If you want your wishes to be legally binding, however, you must weave them into a trust instrument, typically as a Statement of Purpose. You can set forth sufficiently broad general principles as to provide a trustee discretion in administering a trust when unforeseen circumstances arise, but specific enough to express goals for your offspring. Otherwise, your letter of instructions is not legally binding.

Further Thoughts on Wealth Transfer Planning

MOST IMPORTANT, DON'T make permanent plans. Consider only the next five years. Many things may change over that time frame. Your assets may change. There will likely be additions to (and subtractions from) your family through marriages, births, divorces, and deaths. Your wishes may change. In short, try to make plans for the next five years, instead of thinking decades ahead.

Review your plans every five years, sooner if there are any changes in circumstances, such as marriages, births, divorces, or deaths. A plan is only final if you: make outright gifts to others; place property into an irrevocable trust; become mentally incapacitated; or die. Otherwise, anything else can be changed.

Don't wait for the perfect plan. No single wealth transfer plan is right for you. Try to strike a balance among your goals, your family's needs, and tax considerations. Without getting into a detailed discussion about federal estate taxation (see Chapter 10), which is fairly easy to reduce for most estates, often there will be a trade-off between giving up control of your property now, distributions (leaving everything to your spouse), and tax savings. As discussed in this chapter, you must also decide whether to give assets during your lifetime or leave assets to your children (or grandchildren) outright on your death, or create a trust with restrictions designed to protect your wealth from their mistakes. A good estate planner will present alternatives to you. Each possibility will resolve the trade-offs differently.

9 Suggestions for Handling Family Business Succession

Eric Williams is the founder and CEO of Williams Corp., a successful plastic products firm doing about $30 million in sales annually. Eric is now sixty-six and thinking about slowing down, perhaps working only seven or eight months a year or less, but he is reluctant to stop completely. Eric's oldest child, Sophie, is a medical resident; his middle child, John, is studying law. Neither has any interest in running the family business. His youngest, Alice, is still in college working toward a BA in business administration, but she is only twenty years old.

Currently, the firm's chief operating officer, Peter, a nonfamily member who has been with the company for fifteen years, appears talented and ambitious. Eric worries that if he doesn't make Peter the CEO, Peter will get impatient and leave before Alice is ready and experienced enough to take over the reins.

On the other hand, he also worries that as CEO, Peter may sell off some of the assets or go off into other product lines that Eric doesn't believe will successfully integrate with the company's basic products.

If you own a business, you must consider whether or not you want it to remain in your family and last for generations. The odds aren't good on the survival of a family business, one in which a family (for purposes of this chapter, you and your spouse) effectively controls the firm's strategic direction and from which the family derives significant income, wealth, or identity in the community (or industry). Only 12 to 15 percent of all family businesses reach the third generation—your grandchildren.

Apart from taxes, family businesses do not survive for many reasons, including technological changes, heightened competition, regulations, shifts in the economy, or just bad luck. Others do not survive because no family member is interested in running them or is capable of managing them. Stories abound about family businesses that failed because of unresolved family conflicts.

Like Eric Williams, you've made tremendous investments of time and money to build a successful family business. There's often a lot at stake: personal well-being, financial security, and status in the community. It will require considerable effort to ensure that your enterprise survives as a family business, if that is what you desire.

The survival of a family business presents a simple mathematical dilemma. If the founder has two children, and they, in turn, have several children each, within a few generations there may be a number of people looking for highly compensated positions in the entity, assuming it remains successful. The number of competing parties, each of whom owns part of the firm's equity, may make it impossible to reach a workable consensus on key business issues, including the criteria for entering and exiting management and/or ownership of the business and the role family members play in running the organization.

You must deal with your family members' concerns and needs—emotional and financial—as well as your own. Trouble ensues if you cannot mesh business goals with your personal objectives, as well as those of your family members. If the succession plan does not meet the business goals, the enterprise will not be properly run and will likely fail. Instead of working harmoniously for the business, your children and grandchildren may spend their time fighting.

The health of your family's relationships forms a key human aspect to the success or failure of any succession plan. You must consider whether your family members are a cohesive group made up of members who respect one another, listen to and consider different viewpoints, and are able to arrive at a decision all can live with.

The opening scenario of this chapter offers a road map for decision-making, presenting three key questions (and a number of sub-questions) for your consideration:

1. Are you prepared to formulate and implement a succession plan?
2. Do you want your business to survive and be run by one or more family members?
3. What role do you see for yourself in the business after you implement a succession plan?

Unlike other chapters in this book, this chapter poses numerous questions for you to ponder due to the number of variables. Also discussed are family dysfunctionalities, the need to separate ownership from management, and strategies for the transition period.

Question #1

ARE YOU PREPARED to formulate and implement a succession plan? Are you willing to turn over management of the company you worked hard to build to your children (or nonfamily members)? Or, are you procrastinating due to your insecurity about retirement, mortality, or personal finances?

Conceptualizing a plan will force you to acknowledge that you are not indispensable and must at some point make managerial and ownership changes. If you make yourself indispensable, the business may not have much value (apart from its real estate and inventory) to a family member or an outsider.

You must deal with power and control issues. Many founding business owners want to continue to control their firms. Being protective of their authority, they often do not want to cede control, viewing the business as another child and safeguard it accordingly. Having a strong emotional tie to the firm, the business personifies their self-image and ego. Are you emotionally attached to your company? Can the business survive without you? Many entrepreneurs are more emotionally attached to something they created than what has been inherited from a previous generation.

Sergio was fiercely protective of the consulting firm he founded. He controlled all the decisions about both the client services the business provided and the operation of the office. His controlling and sometimes volatile nature drove his children to seek employment elsewhere.

In the typical family business, all decisions flow from founder and owner, such as Sergio, who dominates everything. Secrecy prevails with little or no information flowing down from the top. There is an absence of objective input into decision-making. The founder-owner is told whatever everyone expects that he or she wants to hear. Does this describe your business?

Question #2

ASSUMING THAT YOU now (or in the near future) want to begin the planning process, do you want your business to continue as a family business? If so, can and will it survive? Or, do you want to cash out and sell the business during your lifetime or on your death?

Let's start with the sale option first. Carol established a thriving wine merchandising business knowing full well that neither her children nor her siblings had any interest in doing more than sampling the wine. From the outset, Carol planned to sell the business and leave her heirs the proceeds. Prior to selling to outsiders, an owner, such as Carol, may want to give long-term employment contracts to family members. However, a buyer, wanting to make his or her own staffing choices, will likely resist.

If your business is large enough, you may want to consider the sale of equity to outsiders via an initial public offering (IPO) or a private equity investment. These actions typically impose new demands and lead to the creation of new structures. Preparing for an IPO or a private equity transaction may require you to fire your children and restructure your board, bringing in outside directors.

The equity obtained from a sale may enable your family to exit an industry in decline. The sale proceeds, if large enough, often constitute a new family asset, resulting in money management becoming the new family business.

However, a decision not to continue the entity as a family business raises a whole other series of questions beyond the scope of this chapter, such as what will happen to your children, especially those who depend on the business for livelihood? Also, are you concerned that following a sale, a shift in your firm's "corporate culture" may occur? Many laid back or family-friendly small firms become more profit-driven and stressful when taken over by outsiders.

Let's assume that you want to implement a plan to transition the management and ownership of your business to your children and/or grandchildren. If your business name isn't a random word (such as Yahoo! or Google), but instead your family name (such as Trump or Marriott), you may want your company to remain a memorial to yourself. Be honest with yourself: Do you have a dynastic commitment to continue the family business carrying your name?

In addition to your motivation and your understandable desire to leave a legacy, timing plays a key role. Do you want to leave the business? If so, when? Or, do you want to "die in the saddle," with succession taking place after your death?

You should begin to plan at least five years before you intend to move on, while you are still healthy. Starting early by planning five years out gives your family members time to adjust to the new arrangement. You will need at least one family member who is willing and able to run the business, and five years gives you time to select, groom, and test a successor.

Open and honest discussion is key. Candidly discuss your ideas for your family and your firm. However, don't push your children to participate in planning for the firm's future stability and growth.

Are there one or more family members now involved in the business? What are each one's abilities and skills? Are they business savvy? If they are currently involved, are they interested in managing the enterprise someday?

Frank had a successful national retail chain worth hundreds of millions of dollars. He had two daughters who were competent and very involved in the business. Frank's greatest concern was that, since childhood, the two had fought over everything from dolls to corporate office space. His wife often joked that they couldn't even agree on when to have dinner.

If there is more than one family member involved in the business, are they both competent? Do significant differences exist in their interests, abilities, skills, and energy levels? Are they equally talented? Or, do they possess complementary abilities and skills? How do they get along? Does goodwill presently exist between (or among) them? What is the likelihood of future cooperation between (or among) them? Will they resort to familial warfare? Are they able to collaborate and work as a team in managing the business? Do they now have (or what is the likelihood that they will have) conflicting goals with respect to running the business? Will they be able to manage conflict in their business relationship? Do you act unilaterally with respect to the business so that the next generation lacks a sound model for collaboration?

Remember: Siblings, such as Frank's two daughters, who do not currently get along likely will make poor managers when running the business falls to them. They may pursue different agendas: one or more may want to cash out, while others may wish to continue to build the business.

Are your children's in-laws involved in the business? Is an in-law kept on despite any real interest and ability? Or, is a talented in-law blocked from taking over by a child who is in the business, but is not as capable?

In the 1960s, Fred, a Texas oil wildcatter, struck it rich and built a successful regional petroleum refining business. Many were surprised when he suddenly died at age 51, but they were shocked when his wife, Sally, who until then had been a full-time homemaker, stepped forward and took over the business. Not only did she manage the existing business, but she built it up to a much greater level over the next twenty-five years of her presidency and eventually took it public. Almost no one knew that Fred had been quietly discussing every important business decision with Sally when he came home each evening, grooming her as a possible successor.

What will your spouse's role be if she or he survives you? Can your surviving spouse manage the business? If your children will manage the business, how will you provide for your surviving spouse? As to your surviving spouse's future role in the business, differences exist depending on whether your spouse is or is not the parent of your children. If not the biological parent, her or his concern may only be an assurance of income for the rest of her or his life.

If your adult children are not involved in the business, you need to determine whether they wish to be. Ask each to write out 1) what his or her goals for the business are, and 2) the extent of his or her future involvement. Can you come up with one child who could manage the business? Ask yourself: Does anyone possess the interest and the ability to maintain profitability? Carefully assess your children and their spouses. Become aware of each of your children's (and their spouses') capabilities, limitations, and weaknesses. Consider their relative ages. Do you doubt a daughter's business acumen, overlooking her in favor of a less competent son (or son-in-law)?

Could the business be operated on a co-equal basis by two (or more) of your children who are not presently involved in the business? Can the siblings make shared decisions?

If one (or more) of your offspring are considering a future as your successor, he, she, or they must demonstrate involvement, commitment, and ability. This generally takes years.

Are you willing to delegate authority and responsibility to the next generation in preparation for the succession? If so, whether or not a family member-successor is currently involved in the business, you need to train and develop a child (or in-law) so that he or she obtains the skills needed to manage significant responsibilities and be compensated accordingly. You must implement an adequate training and development program for your successor.

If there is a potential successor, you must delegate authority and responsibility to him or her. Set up a training and development program for him or her, including control over a function or a line of business so that he or she gains confidence in decision-making. Begin by delegating responsibility, authority, and accountability to the one designated to shoulder the ongoing management duties. He, she, or they need to learn to deal with the difficulties and obligations of running a business and to work smoothly with nonfamily member employees.

Warning: Do not groom a successor who lacks the interest and ability to manage your business. Be realistic. You also need to consider whether a potential successor sees the business in noneconomic terms, such as status in the community (or the industry) from involvement in a well-established entity, or a need to continue what you (or prior family members) founded even though that is not what he or she really wants to do.

Accept that your children may not show any interest in working in the family business, never mind running it. Do they have a passion for the business or do they want to follow another path? Do they want to pursue other endeavors that they find bring them more mental and emotional stimulation and provide them with more pleasure?

It may be hard for you to realize that none of your children has the desire or capacity to take over. If you want the business to continue, can an in-law run it or will it be necessary to bring in an outsider? Will one or more experienced nonfamily members be brought in to manage (or help manage) the business, with family members retaining part or full ownership? Will family members resent the presence of nonfamily members in top managerial roles, especially if your business has operated for several generations before outsiders were brought in? Will outsiders be seen as having their own agendas and not having family interests at heart?

Question #3

WHAT ROLE DO you see for yourself in the business after the implementation of the succession plan? Do you want to maintain control of the business even after your retirement? Like Eric Williams in the opening scenario, consider whether you will gradually phase out of management and control or go to full retirement on one specific day.

Even if your ego and personality are bound up with the business, you need to prepare to turn over the reins psychologically, including developing other interests outside the business. You must prepare yourself emotionally for the transition and ultimately for retirement. At the next social gathering, can you be comfortable with no longer telling people you are the president of a company, but instead are babysitting for your grandchildren? Although the enterprise is likely a large part of your identity, you need to redefine yourself.

Your withdrawal, partial or total, from the business will likely create a vacuum not only in the organization but also in your life. Finding yourself without an anchor, you may meddle with managerial activities and your successor's decisions. You may physically leave but symbolically remain, thereby thwarting any succession plan. You need to find other challenges outside the business. Is there another activity you can transition to on your retirement?

What will be your financial profile on withdrawing from managing the business? What kind of retirement income do you and your spouse desire? How much money will you need from the business to support your lifestyle? If you continue to retain control, as chairman of the board of directors, for example, in order to maintain your cash flow from the business, you will likely prevent the successful implementation of a succession plan. In addition to transferring and thereby losing power, are you able to give up the perks you have acquired?

An experienced attorney can suggest various strategies for turning ownership of an illiquid business into an asset that can provide a stream of income so that you can retire with financial security. These include a stock redemption plan so that your firm can buy back your shares or a funded salary continuation agreement so you will receive a guaranteed income for a stated period.

Dealing with Family Dysfunctionalities

A NUMBER OF family-oriented questions must be addressed in formulating and implementing a succession plan. Long-standing, often dormant, family conflicts pose difficult, sometimes intractable, problems. Differences in ages and attitudes among your children often intensify these challenges.

Sibling rivalry, which results from your children competing for your approval, enters into the picture. Each of your children typically desires to obtain your approval and love. Each seeks to do more than his or her siblings and thereby collect more of the love available from you (and your spouse). Rivalry may exist in the conflicts of two or more children who are (or wish to be) active in the business.

When Martha planned for her successors, she had to consider her three children: two were already active in the business, although one was more levelheaded and patient, while the other was somewhat prone to temper tantrums and occasionally rash decisions. While she planned for all three of them to be involved, her youngest had drifted in and out of college, never completing his undergraduate degree. He had been arrested a few times and once was briefly incarcerated for drug use. She knew he had always felt less loved than his older siblings and feared that he would sink deeper into alcohol or drugs if he were not somehow included with the others.

Choosing one sibling to lead the business in the next generation is difficult for you and your children, as it was for Martha. It may be an agonizing choice. Favoring one child over others in the succession plan, and thereby concentrating leadership in him or her, may create the very familial conflicts you seek to avoid. Designating a successor can trigger feelings of jealously toward him or her, often exacerbating sibling rivalry. You must be able to articulate diplomatically why one or more children were not chosen.

If several family members are available to fill leadership positions, their ability to manage as a team may, however, be impeded by competition among them. Make certain they can work well together and clearly define their roles.

Conflicts also arise in the disparate needs and desires of family members active in the business and those who are not.

The Need to Separate Ownership from Management

THOMAS WAS THE founder-owner of a small but very profitable financial investment services firm. His only child, Jay, had a lot of work experience in this field, but had lost his securities license and narrowly avoided jail time by repaying a client from whom he had "borrowed" a large amount of money. Thomas really didn't trust Jay to manage the business, but he did want him to enjoy an income from it. His ownership succession plan differs from a management succession arrangement. Ownership succession may also have a different timetable than management succession.

You need to decide not only who will run your business, but also who will have voting and ownership rights and who will receive future income from the entity. Assuming that you want to transfer ownership to the next generation, to dispel unrealistic expectations, you need to educate the future owners about the responsibilities of ownership, including financial disclosures to shareholders, fiduciary obligations, and formalizing a distribution policy for the enterprise.

You also must decide how and when you will transfer ownership, by the gift of your interest, the sale, or a combination of gift and sale. Your future financial needs from the business may limit how (and particularly, when) you can transfer ownership. The future financial needs of your children and grandchildren will also impact on possible transfer techniques.

You likely have an instinctive desire to treat all of your children equally by giving each an equal ownership share of the business, whether or not they are active in the business. Dividing the business equally among active and inactive children may result in or heighten sibling rivalry. Why? Inactive children may look to the business as a source of income but are often excluded from participation in business decisions. This leads to conflict between the active children, who want compensation income and the reinvestment of profits in the business, and the inactive children, who want distributions and various forms of non-compensation income, including overgenerous salaries for little or no productive work so they can continue to enjoy a "cushy" lifestyle.

There are more than a few family-owned businesses with an empty office held for the inactive offspring who may wander in only once or twice a year. The active children may see the inactives as parasites, while the inactive children view the actives as plunderers. Also, if your children do not get along (and you now mediate their disputes), giving them equal voting power over the business likely will not lead to an amicable arrangement. You may want to consider some type of differential voting rights approach.

You may want to transfer ownership of the business to a successor who will run the business and give different assets to your other children. You can designate that your personal and real estate assets (home, vacation home, etc.) go to one child (or children) and the business to the child who is active in the enterprise. If your business consists of the bulk of your estate, consider using life insurance. Life insurance allows you to leave your business to the child who runs it, but leave others an equal inheritance. Your children who are not involved in the business will receive the life insurance proceeds. This plan assumes, of course, that your health allows a sufficient amount of coverage at reasonable rates. The life insurance policies could be placed in an irrevocable insurance trust to avoid its being taxed in your estate.

Strategies for the Transition Period

DURING THE TRANSITION period, it is better for you, as the founder, while alive, in consultation with family members, not only to implement a plan for management and ownership succession but also to delineate guiding principles for your firm.

Ask yourself: Have you used your business to build the self-esteem and maturity of your children, to nurture them into responsible adults, and to provide for them financially? Or, has your business served as a family welfare organization in which you hire or put on the payroll weak and unproductive family members? Does the firm provide jobs for your children, many of whom lack business interest, skills, or energy? Do your children feel that as family members they are entitled to financial benefits from the business and that they need not heed any directive or do any productive work? These unresolved, dormant family issues, such as a sense of entitlement from the enterprise, must be addressed by you, and not left to a successor, whether a child or a nonfamily member.

Your business ought not be an employer of last resort for your children. Reserving promotions and top management positions for family members, regardless of merit, not only breeds mediocrity but is also unfair to nonfamily employees and managers who make significant contributions to the business.

Reevaluate the compensation and benefits paid to family members. Some children may be underpaid relative to peers in similar positions at other companies in the industry, or, more likely, they may be overpaid.

Even before you leave the business, your firm needs objective, written rules, guidelines, and agreements on key personnel issues, such as hiring, compensation, retention, and promotion. For example, family members who work in the business ought to obtain compensation, benefits, and promotions based on performance and responsibility, not family status. Compensation and benefits for family members ought to be realistic for the jobs being done. More generally, human resources policies must be similar to what family members would be required to meet in the employment market. You want to create, in so far as is possible, objective standards for family members and enforce these standards.

You need to deal with family members who are underperformers, have not kept up with industry trends, or have limited experience as a result of spending their entire career in the family business. Are incompetent family members employed at exorbitant salaries, thereby dampening the incentive for and the retention of skilled, contributing family members and nonfamily employees? Help your designated successor by weeding out any inbred incompetents before you turn over the reins.

Consider also your company's board of directors. Typically it includes the firm's major shareholders, such as yourself, key family member executives, and managers. Has your business grown so that your firm needs outside expertise (and possibly some key nonfamily member managers) on your board? If so, invite experienced outsiders to serve on your board. They provide useful insights into day-to-day management and strategic decision-making. They also help you balance the compensation and benefits for children active in the business; the distributions desired by inactive children; and the cash needs of the business for working capital and expansion. They hopefully will be able to advise your successors, the future managers and owners, on the best ways to keep the firm successful.

Further Thoughts on Business Succession Planning

INVOLVE YOUR ADULT children in the business succession planning process. But limit the discussion of certain key topics, such as management and/or ownership succession, to those directly involved.

You don't want your successor to be surprised at the reading of your will, finding him or her suddenly the president of an ongoing business. Involving the next generation in the planning process may enable them to come up with ideas you have not considered. Their involvement may give you an opportunity to assess their problem-solving skills and their ability to collaborate. It also offers the next generation a voice on matters of importance to their lives and careers. Once you take care of the personal and family issues, the legal work, whether through wills, trusts, buy-sell agreements, and funding (e.g., through life insurance), becomes easier.

Before you implement any plan, get input from family members on the general outline of your succession plan. Begin by communicating the outline of your plan to family members. Doing this as soon as possible enables the potential conflicts and resentment to surface, be discussed, and be resolved before you finalize and implement your plan.

For successful business succession planning, you will need a team of trusted advisors: an attorney who specializes in business and estate planning for family firms and a business consultant having experience with entities of your type and size. You may also need a facilitator, who has family therapy training, to help address the emotional issues that arise around succession planning.

If you don't decide the management and ownership succession issues well in advance while you are active and healthy, you almost guarantee that the business and/or amicable family relationships will not survive for many years after you leave the firm.

10 Creating and Leaving a Legacy

Warren Buffett is one of the richest men in America. While his children have benefited from being born and raised in great affluence, their father has made it very well known to his family and the general public that the bulk of his wealth will go to charities, mainly the Gates Foundation.

The more wealth you have, the more options exist for you. For some, it means leaving their wealth to their children and grandchildren. Others plan to leave few, if any, assets to their children, especially if their offspring are well off and do not need additional funds. Or, they may opt for this route because they think their children will only waste any assets left to them. Others want to provide extensively for their grandchildren whom they feel may face greater obstacles than their children.

As you think about formulating your wealth transmission plans, start by identifying your lifetime needs and the sources that will provide for these needs. Of course, include your spouse's needs as well. Only after estimating your lifetime spending needs and income sources can you plan for the amounts you want to give to your offspring or charity, now and in the future. The size of the cushion you personally want will impact your lifetime and death-time plans.

In formulating your plans, you need to consider your goals. Weigh your preference among various alternatives, including your future standard of living, how much you want to give to loved ones, what you want to leave to charity, or pay in federal estate taxes. If you have sufficient wealth, beyond maintaining financial independence for you (and your spouse), what is your primary goal, for instance, preserving your lifestyle under any number of possible scenarios, or scaling back your standard of living, now and in the future, so you can provide more to your children (and grandchildren) or charity? Or, do you want to focus on the most likely scenario and just add a modest cushion to cover any surprises?

Albert constantly gave more and more money to his idle playboy son, bailing him out of many financial scrapes, but when Albert died, he left the bulk of his estate to his hardworking daughter who had quietly endured being on the sidelines of his largesse during his lifetime.

Like Albert, you may face a key estate planning question if you want to leave the bulk of your assets to your children and grandchildren. Is equal treatment of paramount concern to you? Or, do you regard one child (or grandchild) as needier or more deserving than others, because, for example, he or she serves as a caregiver for another family member? Sometimes the needier child is offended at being treated as a "charity" case. Leaving unequal shares to your loved ones may be viewed, probably quite likely, as an expression of your approval of some and disapproval of others.

By the time he was ten years old, Carl's parents had sent him off to a European boarding school. He harbored great resentments about being ignored although given every advantage imaginable. He never forgave his parents for sending him away and, despite marrying a wealthy woman, his mission in life after his parents died seemed to be squandering his inheritance.

Is there a maximum amount you feel each of your children and grandchildren should inherit, concluding that beyond this ceiling any excess would negatively impact on their character, lessening self-esteem or undermining ambition? If so, you may want to give your children and grandchildren "enough" money for them to be "comfortable." Each of us, of course, has his or her own definition of what is "enough" and what is a "comfortable" lifestyle. A child's need and character enter into the decision. A larger wealth transfer ought to go to a child with greater need, for example, if disabled, or one with a strong character, who has established him- or herself independently.

Whatever you decide to do with respect to wealth transfer planning, communicate your decision, in general terms, to your older teens and adult children, while you are alive. Be certain that you and your spouse are on the same page. If you are not in agreement, perhaps each of you ought to plan separately but revisit your decisions in five years.

Tell your older teens and adult children about your hopes, dreams, and fears for each of them; what you want and what you expect from each. Explain your beliefs about how each will use your wealth shaped the form and manner of your plan.

For your older teens and adult children, tell them what they can expect from you financially and when, now, in the future, on your (or your spouse's) death. You'll likely promise that they can obtain college and graduate school degrees, debt-free. You may also promise: presents for graduation and a wedding, a down payment on a house, or seed money for a business. You need to set realistic expectations about what will come from you and what will come from them. You want your children to get a great education. However, you may want to provide more help in buying a house than paying for an expensive wedding.

Explain your reasons and let your children have an opportunity to express their thoughts. Articulate your plans to avoid misunderstandings. Let them know generally what is in your plan. Otherwise, feelings will be hurt if they are surprised after your death. Their anger or bitterness may be taken out on others. If you're not going to treat your children equally, let them know ahead of time. Let them be mad with you now when you have the opportunity to explain your reasons.

If you have funded (see the discussion of 529 plans, Chapter 7, pages 120–123) or paid for the education expenses of your children and grandchildren, do you want to give away a large part of your wealth to charity, now or in the future, subject to keeping enough to maintain your standard of living?

Federal estate and state inheritance taxes enter into the picture. The federal estate tax is imposed on property you transfer at death. The estate pays the tax, thereby reducing the amount of assets your loved ones receive.

Consult an experienced estate planning attorney who will help you understand what the word "estate" means for federal estate tax purposes. As you will learn, the term "estate" is very broad.

As you are probably aware, you can transfer an unlimited amount of property on your death to your spouse who is a U.S. citizen. You do this tax-free transfer through the federal estate tax marital deduction. You and your spouse also each have an exemption amount, technically, the applicable exclusion amount, from the federal estate tax. The gift tax credit used against your lifetime taxable gifts (see Chapter 7, page 122) reduces the credit (the applicable exclusion amount) available for your estate to use against your federal estate tax liability. Again, your estate planner will help you structure your estate to take maximum advantage of the estate tax marital deduction, if you are married, and the exemption amount.

For high net worth individuals, once your advisor tells you about the top federal estate tax rate (and state inheritance taxes), you may not want to leave millions of dollars in your estate to be taxed. This will likely lead you to consider making charitable gifts.

Question: Are you interested in dedicating a significant portion of your wealth to charity?

Charitable Giving

IF YOU DO not want to give or leave all your money to your children and grandchildren, consider philanthropy as a way to create and build a legacy. Altruism may motivate your charitable giving. You may want to give back to one or more charitable organization(s). Taxes, of course, enter into the picture as does a desire for prestige, recognition, and to be remembered.

Consider the charitable organizations with which you have had some connection during your lifetime. Have you had ongoing relationships, such as volunteering, serving as a trustee, attending annual events, or simply donating money on a regular basis to one or more nonprofit entities? These involvements may predispose you to be generous, but it is important that you ask some key questions before deciding how much and in what form to make your charitable transfers.

First, does the organization's mission mesh with your interests? Some organizations may appear on the surface to align with your interests, but examine their activities and what they actually fund. Secondly, is the charity run in a professional manner, with reasonable administrative costs? Thirdly, can the organization be expected to continue well into the future? One well-intentioned Holocaust survivor left a very substantial amount to an organization committed to only supporting survivors such as herself. Since most of these people are over seventy, it is unlikely that the organization will continue far into the future (or it will need to recast its mission).

You must decide whether to make charitable contributions now, over a period of years, or on your death through your will or a trust. You may want to begin by making current gifts to see if one charity (or a small group of charities) should receive larger, subsequent gifts. You may find that the charity is not as efficient as you thought or does not allocate its spending in ways you prefer. Once you make an outright charitable gift it is out of your hands.

You may want to think beyond giving money or property outright to a charity now or through your will or a trust. You should check with your charitable organizations to see whether they offer formal, planned giving arrangements and work with their (and your) advisors.

Ruth loved piano music all her life and had experienced success as a concert pianist. Her family readily accepted that she established a program to support and encourage young composers and performers and to provide pianos for university music departments. As a wealthy widow, Ruth sought out an advisor who presented her with various strategies that would allow her to retain more control than an outright gift. Like Ruth, these techniques can provide you, your spouse, or your loved ones tax benefits and in some instances with income for a period of years. Let's consider four alternative charitable giving strategies: a private foundation; a donor-advised fund; a charitable reminder trust; and a charitable gift annuity. A charitable lead trust is beyond the scope of this book.

Private Foundations

YOU CAN CREATE a private philanthropic entity, organized as a tax-exempt trust or a corporation, set its purpose, and select the initial trustees or board of directors. While you are alive, you can designate how the foundation makes distributions for charitable purposes.

You receive a federal income (or federal estate) tax deduction for contributions to fund the foundation. The income tax deduction is subject to an annual percentage limit and may be subject to additional limitations, depending on the type of property contributed. Consult your tax advisor for details.

A private foundation can, if you wish, help your family. It appeals to donors who wish to use charitable giving to teach their offspring lovingkindness (Virtue 5) through service as well as stewardship. For example, by specifying a limited set of charitable purposes, such as giving to arts organizations, a donor can teach his or her children to appreciate the arts.

If building character and influencing behavior are key goals, you can designate family members as the trustees or directors. Family members so selected help run the foundation, with the privilege and responsibility of determining the charitable recipients. Family members can also be employed by the foundation. In addition to drawing reasonable salaries and reimbursement of expenses, they build their own legacies and can learn to work together.

A private foundation helps younger loved ones. You can encourage your children and grandchildren over the age of ten or so to research grantees. You can take your children and grandchildren on field trips to see grantees (and potential grantees) in action.

By involving your children and grandchildren in the management of the foundation's assets, they likely will receive an education in investment management. Teens can learn how stock markets work and investment portfolios are constructed. Other useful skills include how to create a budget, allocate resources, and reach decisions.

Private foundations offer leadership opportunities,

apart from service as trustees or directors. You may want each of your children and grandchildren on reaching age twenty-one to have the opportunity to serve on an advisory board that helps decide how to spend the foundation's assets. Involvement in a foundation also educates young adults on the difficulties potential grantees face in fund-raising, continuing operations, and implementing programs.

In sum, besides creating a legacy and helping grant recipients, a private foundation enables you to teach valuable life and business skills, including developing budgets, measuring returns on investments, selecting and monitoring recipients, to your family members. It encourages responsibility on the part of your offspring and may help give their life meaning.

Negatives, however, abound. You need to fund a private foundation with at least $5 million. In addition to start up costs, there are ongoing maintenance and compliance costs, including significant annual fees for administration and investment management, and a federal excise tax on investment income. Creating a private foundation is not only expensive but also time-consuming, as it requires IRS approval. There are ongoing swamps of paperwork and annual IRS filings, which are subject to public disclosure. There is no anonymity in the grantmaking.

Because of the expenses for a staff to operate the foundation, you probably need to give $10 million or more. Paying the salary for a full-time or part-time executive director, who sets budgets and screens grant proposals, and possibly hiring an office administrator, however, frees family members to examine prospective grantees, make site visits, and focus on the entity's greater vision.

A foundation may become a source of dissension among you and your children, or among your children (or grandchildren) when you and your spouse are gone. Disagreements may arise about the foundation's mission or its grant-making priorities. Even if you craft a mission statement that will crystallize your goals for the foundation and help guide its grantmaking, things may change during your grandchildren's and great-grandchildren's lifetimes.

You need to focus on a foundation's duration. Forever is a long time. The foundation may become a self-serving vehicle for those who run it. Also, to avoid future mission drift, marked by a shift in the foundation's goals and its grant recipients, you may want to limit the entity's life span through a sunset provision, for example, mandating that the foundation spend its endowment within a specified time period.

Donor-Advised Funds

DONOR-ADVISED FUNDS, AS public charities, are set up by financial services firms or charitable organizations, such as higher education institutions or community foundations. They are basically investment pools that act as intermediaries between donors and charities, usually allowing benefactors to play a role in how their donations are invested.

With a donor-advised fund, you make an irrevocable contribution to the fund and can decide in subsequent years which charities will receive gifts. Thus, similar to a private foundation, a donor-advised fund lets you and your family consolidate and manage your philanthropy, now and for years to come. You can make a one-time gift or spread your contributions over a period of years.

You receive a current federal income tax deduction, subject to an annual percentage limitation, and a five-year carryover for any excess deductions, for your lifetime contributions to the fund or a federal estate tax deduction for a deathtime contribution.

You can transfer cash, appreciated securities, and real property (the latter only if allowed by the sponsoring fund). Sophie and Dale had owned a modest beach bungalow for over forty years in what had recently become a very popular vacation spot, but which no longer suited these retirees or any of their family. A donor-advised fund makes sense for individuals, such as Sophie and Dale, donating appreciated property because they can take advantage of the maximum federal income tax breaks for such gifts. When you donate appreciated property held for more than one year, you will not be subject to the federal capital gains tax.

The sponsoring fund invests your contributions. Because the fund is tax exempt, donated assets grow tax-free within your account. Financial services firms and others let you choose how to invest your account, which range from conservative to aggressive, within limits. A trend exists to give donors more investment choices. Some funds will even allow you to select a money manager for your account, but you cannot serve as the manager. For even larger accounts, some funds will design a personalized portfolio, using a mix of individual securities and mutual funds. Although you preserve the ability to make, more accurately recommended, investments and charitable gifts, legally you relinquish control over the assets you contribute to the fund.

You decide when all or part of the account is to be donated to various charities and what charities will receive the distributions. The fund handles the administrative details. You decide how much to give, when to make a gift, and who will receive a gift. You can decide to postpone substantial grants from your account until your account's tax free returns (perhaps combined with further contributions) have generated sufficient growth to make larger grants possible.

You can support several charities simultaneously. Thus, a donor-advised fund is useful for people who wish to divide money among various charitable recipients. As the donor, you can be identified or remain anonymous, unlike a private foundation that cannot give anonymously.

A donor-advised fund has a simplified setup, record keeping, and administration. You need only fill out an application and make a contribution equal to or greater than the fund's initial minimum, which may be as low as $5,000. A donor-advised fund avoids a private foundation's significant up-front setup costs. The manager also administers the fund, files any tax reports, and prepares statements. Your account is subject to annual investment and administrative fees totaling roughly 1.5 to 2 percent of the balance. These ongoing fees are typically lower than those for a private foundation. Depending on your situation, you may be better off skipping the fees and giving the gifts out annually. However, giving directly to a number of charities requires sorting through each year's worth of charitable receipts for federal income tax purposes.

With a donor-advised fund you can make philanthropy part of your legacy. By designating your adult children and grandchildren as advisors to the fund, they learn the lessons of service and stewardship just as if they were involved with a family foundation.

You can also designate one or more individuals as successors for your account after your death, thereby enabling your children and grandchildren to make grants thereafter. By naming loved ones advisors and/or successors, you establish a charitable tradition, helping create future generations of philanthropists.

Rather than a traditional college graduation gift, you may want to fund a donor-advised fund for each of your offspring. This type of gift will enable them to get involved in philanthropy by researching and making grants to charities of their choice. They can start with small amounts before moving on to more ambitious charitable projects, if they choose.

In sum, donor-advised funds are popular because they are private, require less paperwork (and thus, offer lower expenses), and provide better federal income tax breaks than a private foundation. Consult your tax advisor. One negative. Unlike a private foundation, a donor does not have the satisfaction (and accompanying headaches) of running an independent entity.

Charitable Remainder Trusts

EVA WAS SEVENTY-FIVE years old when she donated shares

of stock that had appreciated in value over a number of years to her favorite charity through a charitable remainder trust. In return she received an annual income, guaranteed until her death. Additionally, she was able to claim a substantial income tax deduction for the year in which she made the gift.

Charitable remainder trusts are popular among affluent donors who want to make charitable gifts. With this type of trust, a donor-settlor irrevocably gives cash, appreciated securities or real estate to a living or testamentary trust. The trust pays income to the donor (or someone else the donor designates) as the beneficiary. The income may be payable for life or a fixed term of years, not to exceed twenty years. Thus, a charitable remainder trust created during life enables the donor to build a legacy, while avoiding the risk that he or she will give away too much wealth, provided the donor designates him- or herself as the trust beneficiary. After the income payments end, either on the donor's (or another's) death or after a period of years has passed, the charity receives the trust's remaining assets.

Although the Internal Revenue Code places a floor on the amount of income the donor (or the designated beneficiary) must receive annually, the amount can be: 1) fixed by the trust document or as a percentage of assets when the trust is created; or 2) a percentage of the value of the trust assets to be determined each year. The first option, fixed dollar payments from the trust, offers the prospect of stable income. The beneficiary knows what he or she will receive. However, if the investment returns cannot support the fixed amount, the trust may run out of money and the donor-beneficiary may find him- or herself short of income if he or she lives longer than expected or his or her financial circumstances unexpectedly change. The second method affords more flexibility. By factoring in the future appreciation, this alternative may offer an inflation hedge with respect to future income payments.

By funding a charitable remainder trust during your lifetime (but not on your death), you receive a federal income tax deduction for the present value of the gift that will ultimately go to the charity. The greater the anticipated payout to the income beneficiary, the smaller the remaining principal (more technically, the remainder) going to charity and thus the charitable income tax deduction. The deduction is subject to an annual percentage limit with a five-year carryover. Federal income taxes are payable on the receipt of the income from the trust. Because the trust's assets are not included in your estate, if you are the trust's sole income beneficiary, no federal estate taxes are owed these assets. If you are not the trust's sole income beneficiary, federal estate taxes may be due, subject to the remainder interest qualifying the estate tax charitable deductions, if the other recipient or a successor recipient survives you. Advantageous special estate tax rules exists if your spouse is the only noncharitable beneficiary, other than you. Consult your tax advisor for details.

The trustee, typically the charitable beneficiary, manages the trust assets, generally selling the contributed property that has appreciated in value (e.g., real estate), and reinvesting the proceeds. The donor does not owe any federal capital gains tax on the appreciation when he or she transfers the property to the trust or the trust sells the property and reinvests the proceeds.

If the trust's income beneficiary (other than the donor or the donor's spouse) is also the trustee, he or she is charged with investing the trust assets for his or her benefit and that of the charity, thereby helping teach stewardship. For a novice investor-beneficiary, consider providing a cotrustee or designating an investment advisor.

Because of the costs involved in setting up a charitable remainder trust, specifically, the drafting of the trust instrument, you should contribute assets worth at least $250,000 to create this type of charitable vehicle. Depending on who serves as the trustee, there may also be ongoing administrative and investment costs.

Charitable Gift Annuities

MOST PUBLIC CHARITIES offer gift annuities. During his or her lifetime, the donor contributes property to the charity, and, in exchange, the nonprofit provides an income stream for the life of one (or two) designated individual beneficiaries, but in an amount less than a commercial annuity would pay. The interest payments are backed by the charity's assets, leading most donors to favor large, stable nonprofits, such as universities. Unlike a charitable remainder trust, a charitable gift annuity is not required to pay out any minimum or maximum amounts.

The donor receives an immediate federal income tax deduction for the present value of what the charity expects to wind up with after paying out the income stream, based on the life expectancy of the annuitant(s) and the anticipated income payments. The deduction is subject to annual percentage limit, with a five-year carryover. Increased longevity coupled with federal income tax savings serve as powerful reasons for establishing a charitable gift annuity that combines a charitable donation with a lifetime income stream. However, a portion of the annual income payments are subject to federal income taxation. Gift taxes are not due on the transfer of property to the charity; estate taxes are not payable on the donor's demise. Consult your tax advisor.

Further Thoughts on Charitable Giving

PHILANTHROPY TEACHES CHILDREN and grandchildren about what money can do, not what money can buy. When done in conjunction with your children and grandchildren, charitable giving may help bring a family together. You can teach family members the importance of thrift (Virtue 4), lovingkindness through service (Virtue 5), and stewardship.

Your loved ones ought not to be disaffected by a charitable giving plan that diverts significant family assets away from them. Communication is essential. Talk with your children and grandchildren not only about your charitable goals, but also, more generally, about the transmission of wealth and your views on the impact of wealth on behavior. Letting them appreciate your charitable passion will help them understand your motivation.

Using an Ethical Will to Create a Legacy

TO CREATE A legacy, whether or not you embark on a charitable giving program, you should consider leaving an ethical will. This document generally takes the form of a letter to family members and sets forth the virtues you hope they will inherit from you. It reflects who you are, what you care about, your personality and philosophy and what you feel your purpose was in life, your dreams for your family members' futures, and your words of wisdom for them.

An ethical will may be a document in letter or statement form, in digital form, as an audiotape, a DVD, or a video on YouTube or other video-sharing site. The point is to let your offspring know what matters to you. By conveying emotions to loved ones, an ethical will serves as a love letter to family members. Tell them what you want for them, whether in terms of spirituality, religion, devotion to family members, or other goals.

Through this nonlegal document you make a personal statement. You can reveal what has been important in your life, what was missing, and how you expressed your purpose in life. Separate from your will, it can consist of the history of an individual or a family (as a series of important stories, not a mere chronology); lessons you have learned; mistakes you have made; principles you wish to communicate; and guidelines for living. By imparting important life lessons, you transfer wisdom to succeeding generations. Your children and grandchildren may need your wisdom more than any money you leave them.

By describing your favored character traits and your goals in life, you help reinforce these for family members. By providing personal and family information, you help your loved ones overcome the post-death frustration they often encounter from not having been able to learn more about you.

Because it is a highly personal document, no rules exist as to length or topics to be covered. You can speak your wishes into a tape recorder or video record your thoughts. Because these forms are subject to technological change and impermanency, you may want to prepare a written manuscript.

Writing an ethical will may help you prepare a wealth transfer arrangement that reflects your virtues and goals. Because the process will likely force you to articulate the character traits you find desirable, you may want to share the final product with family members during your lifetime. It may help bring your loved ones closer together.

11 Conclusion: Redirecting Negative Character Traits, Attitudes, and Behaviors

D espite your best efforts, your children—whether age eight, seventeen, or thirty-one—may evidence negative character traits. Or, you may be reading this book long after your child's formative years for positive character development. This chapter will help you make midcourse corrections for youngsters and teens, or even later, for adults. It may be time for you to take a new direction in becoming a more successful parent.

The parents of three children, sixteen-year-old Chris, thirteen-year-old Mac, and ten-year-old Matt, struggled with their oldest child's drug use. When Chris was fifteen, they sent him to outpatient rehab; at age sixteen, he was sent to a residential treatment facility, which forced his parents to dip into their own retirement savings plans. Shortly after returning from a costly residential treatment program, thirteen-year-old Mac became curious about his older brother's hidden "treasure." The parents faced an extremely difficult decision: They had to protect their two younger children from drugs in the home, but how could they care for their not yet adult son?

They explained to Chris their dilemma—that they loved him and wanted to help him—but that they absolutely would not tolerate any drugs in their home. They said that if they found any more drugs anywhere on their property, they would send him to boarding school, using his college tuition savings, and he would be on his own after high school. This was truly a case of tough love. When Chris again brought drugs into the family home, they did as they had promised. The lesson was not lost on the curious Mac, who stayed away from drugs completely.

Dealing with Your Eight- or Seventeen-Year-Old

IF YOU SEE that your eight-year-old is an obnoxious junior brat, a self-centered, demanding bundle of wants, or your seventeen-year-old is an entrenched materialist, basking in the age of entitlement, you and your spouse may need to reevaluate your priorities, values, and goals in life. Are you both on the same page in terms of offering your unconditional love (Rule 1, page 20), providing firm discipline and setting clear boundaries (Rule 2, page 21), and learning to say no (Rule 4, page 25)? What character traits are important to you? Do you value material possessions and social status above all else?

If your eight-year-old refuses to clean up his spilled drink and is rude to hired people who come into your home, you have time to make a midcourse correction with that bratty child. It is possible for him or her to learn to delay gratification, handle frustration and failure, build self-esteem (Virtue 1), become more joyful and optimistic (Virtue 2), serene (Virtue 3), hardworking and thrifty (Virtue 4), loving (Virtue 5), forgiving (Virtue 6), and truthful (Virtue 7). It's more difficult, but not impossible, to correct even your seventeen-year-old shopaholic, who habitually demands $900 handbags and $500 shoes. Stop the flow of nonessential "stuff." Explain that you've been remiss and that you want to correct parenting mistakes to give the child a more fulfilling future. Entitlement is harmful; it destroys motivation and lowers self-esteem. Correcting your child, no matter what his or her age, is the only way to equip him or her to live a better life in the future.

Both you and your spouse must be united in giving far less and requiring much more, so that a child, whether eight or seventeen years old, doesn't play one against the other. Otherwise, children see the disagreement between parents and will divide and conquer the objecting parent.

If your child is already a spoiled, whining brat and you recognize it, you may need to change your priorities and, through word and deed, teach your child about what is important in life. Start by taking a look at the way you live. You may need to say "no" to your own material wants, as opposed to needs. Through self-reflection, focus on a general reexamination of your life. You may need to change the direction of your life and, for example, take the focus off the externals, such as fancy cars, designer-label clothes, prestigious schools, which you may have let define you. Your spending behaviors may contradict your values. Don't let your wealth imprison you. Start by minimizing your mindless consumption. Do you need to impress others in your life or to be true to yourself?

Beyond your own life, you and your spouse may need to talk about your children and work out a plan for dealing with them and their negative character traits. Discuss how to speak to your children about developing positive character traits (Chapters 3 and 4), their friends (Chapter 5), their allowances, and, more generally, about your wealth (Chapter 6). However, principled words and even principled deeds without direction—a vision—are often fruitless.

Preparing a Family Mission Statement

BOB AND MARION suddenly inherited a great deal of money. In planning how to use their newfound wealth, they involved their ten- and twelve-year-olds in writing a family mission statement. In effect, this document became a statement of their family's values and what the family as a whole wanted to accomplish with its wealth.

Preparing a family mission statement helps you to develop a vision, and forms the basis for a unified, proactive plan for you and your children. Although formulating a family mission statement takes effort and time to do it right, it will help you to identify what it is in life that matters to you, your spouse, and your children more than anything else—in other words, your beliefs and your virtues, and what you plan to do to achieve these character traits. It will help you make decisions that ring true to your conscience. It will give you a chance to define who you are, and provide a beacon to help you stay on that course.

In addition to reading Chapters 2, 3, and 4, you may want to begin developing a family mission statement by thinking about the people who have been most influential in your life. Why do you admire them? Reflect on the qualities you admire and what qualities you learned from them. Consider the positive character traits and values, such as education, relationships, work, service to community, and cultural and spiritual endeavors, these influential persons advocated and implemented. What negative traits influenced you or convinced you to avoid behaving in a certain way?

Claudine was a chronic liar who frequently accused her daughter of lying throughout the child's formative and teenage years. As she grew older, Claudine's daughter vowed to tell the truth and to refrain from accusing her own children unless she was absolutely certain that they were not telling the truth. However, for the rest of her life, the daughter was extremely sensitive to being told untruths. She formulated a mission statement emphasizing truthfulness.

Over time, make notes and revise the draft. To stay focused on your family mission statement, you may want to revise it regularly—perhaps annually, or every three years—to keep up with changes. Some families plan to review their mission statements on a certain notable date, such as New Year's Day or a birthday or anniversary.

A family mission statement will help you, your spouse, and your children on their journeys through life. Hopefully family members will find that a lot of what they do will relate directly to the family mission statement. Generalities, such as "to be good people," and vague platitudes are not sufficient; a family mission statement must have specifics. Focusing on unchanging virtues, or character traits, is important to long-term family success. Although it must be precise enough to address virtues and goals, it should also remain general enough to cover unforeseen eventualities.

Everyone involved—you, your spouse, and your children—must be committed to following the family mission statement. The process of drafting it is as important as the final product. Everyone must be heard and learn to reach decisions by consensus and that they can do things together.

Additional Suggestions for Dealing with Your Seventeen-Year-Old

YOUR SELF-ABSORBED MATERIALIST, who is constantly partying, has only a passing interest in high school, and is obsessed with popular culture, is going off to college in a year. If you have not already done so, introduce an allowance, even a substantial one, for this child as a three-part money management training tool, to teach spending, saving, and giving, as well as basic financial literacy. (See Chapter 6.) If your child wants something, let him or her save or work for it. Only give what he or she needs. Be ready to deal with anger and guilt designed to manipulate you. In time, he or she will accept that the reign of entitlement is over.

Talk openly about your resources and the responsibilities that come with them. Making your child part of your philanthropic endeavors and creating the notion of giving back may help modify attitudes. One suggestion would be to involve him or her in a community service project, thereby bringing into focus at-risk city teens. You may want to consider establishing an incentive trust (Chapter 8) to reorient your child's behavior and help give a sense of purpose to his or her life. This type of trust gives a child one last chance to change dysfunctional behavior and possibly avoid disinheritance.

Dealing with Your Thirty-One-Year-Old

ONE WIDOW, WHO adores her daughter and her grandchildren, found herself inundated with visits from this family of four for months at a time whenever they needed a place to regroup. As she put it, "I love them all, but I love them better in short visits. I just want my peace and quiet." When the grandmother announced she was moving to a facility limited to those over sixty years of age, her children assumed that she was giving them her house, but she surprised them, sold the home, and used the sale proceeds to purchase her new one-bedroom accommodation and for her future care needs.

Adult children often present more difficult challenges than younger children do, and many of these challenges often relate to money issues. You should worry if an irresponsible, poorly motivated, dependent adult child is habitually in financial straits and on the "gravy train" into his or her late twenties or early thirties. Do you want to continue making gifts, or teach your children to stand on their own?

Even something as minor as a family cell phone plan can raise difficult issues. This type of calling plan makes it less expensive and easy to give an adult child cell phone service, but it also continues to make that adult dependent on his or her parents.

You must counter your adult child's expectation that the money you provide will save him or her from having to work; that your largesse will continue to bail him or her out of problems. The "help" you continue to provide hurts now and in the long run. We know that it's difficult, but let an adult child experience the real world. The best lessons come from life itself.

Thirty-one-year-old Judy was a compulsive shopper living in a very small studio apartment. She continued to buy TVs, multiple cameras, and vast amounts of clothing, storing them in her parents' modest home. As the family home became more cluttered with things they didn't want and which Judy hardly used, her parents finally gave her an ultimatum: Judy had one month to remove all the items or they would dispose of them. Unfortunately, Judy relied on her parents' generally good nature and the fact that their frequent earlier threats had no consequences and failed to take them seriously this time. One month later, all the items were sold on eBay, at a yard sale, or were donated to charity. It was a painful lesson for Judy, but her parents felt better about themselves than they had in all the years of providing storage.

You cannot blame your adult child for not growing up if your behavior has fostered dependency. Accept that you have played a part in that dependency. Then, make clear to your child that while you realize you have played a part in the situation, you will not facilitate things in the future. Unless there is clinical emotional depression, a disability, or substance abuse, among other serious problems, give this child the opportunity to function independently. If he or she is living at home, select a move-out date; cut off or reduce subsidizing an apartment. Also, discuss the situation with your other children, who may be resentful or angry about the focus of your continued financial assistance resting on one child.

For a wayward adult child, consider making outright gifts monthly, not annually, according to predetermined, budgeted needs, with a portion to be spent, another to be saved, and a third part reserved for charity. Demand that accurate records of expenditures be kept. Be ready to follow through. Don't bail him or her out. And despite the indignation offered, don't give in or reward for a partial effort. Stand firm in helping your child make the transition to independence.

Some Suggestions for All of Your Children

FOR ALL YOUR children, but especially your adult children, it may be helpful to follow these four practices. First, express your unconditional love, which is not tied to a child's performance, achievement, or circumstances (Rule 1, page 20). All your children, even as adults, need to know that they are loved regardless of what they do (or did). Your children, particularly late teens and young adults who may have made poor choices in the past, may begin to follow a healthier path if they experience your warmth and affection, your time and commitment, despite their past mistakes. Accept them the way they are. Offer your encouragement and praise, particularly for positive efforts made.

Second, as your children mature, review and revise your rules and boundaries. Shift from being an authority figure to that of an advisor—but only if asked. Don't offer adult children unsolicited advice. Allow your adult children to make choices, accept the consequences, and taste reality, without rescuing them. After a challenging period of being forced to handle problems, a child's strengths will likely emerge from a sink-or-swim situation; he or she will begin to discover untapped competencies and develop his or her potential. Be there for your adult children emotionally, but not financially. If they ask, help them set realistic goals.

Third, build a trusting relationship with your children. Build trust through acceptance, honesty and openness (Virtue 7), not by keeping secrets, denying responsibility, or blaming others. Set an example for your children.

Fourth, focus on healthy communication. Listen to your children, whether eight, seventeen, or thirty-one years old. Avoid criticizing, belittling, or insulting them; show respect for them. Try to remain in the present. Say what you mean.

Remember: A perfect parent does not exist. Don't blame yourself for previously having been too good to your children in material terms or not sufficiently loving and firm in dealing with them. Be hopeful that a new parenting style will work, but don't count on a miracle, especially for children in their late twenties or early thirties.

INDEX

W / X / Y / Z

WITHDRAWAL

For Every
Individual...

Renew by Phone
269-5222

Renew on the Web
www.indypl.org

For General Library Information
please call 275-4100